Read It in the Classroom!

Organizing an Interactive Language Arts Program Grades 4~9

This book is dedicated to the memory of Francis Harry Hart.

Acknowledgments

The ideas in this book have been growing and consolidating during the last three years. As curriculum consultants we have been privileged visitors in many classrooms where teachers and students have shared their work. To all the teachers who have taken risks and field-tested some of those ideas we owe a great debt. To all the students who have given us samples of their writing and drawing, thank you. This is your book — a celebration of your responses to literature.

In particular we would like to name Bruce Singleton and Marge Kelly, who worked through the idea of theme units with us. Bruce also contributed his written account of working on a unit about children during World War II.

We appreciate and acknowledge the expertise in children's literature shared by Judy Sarick and the staff at the Children's Bookstore in Toronto.

Thanks also to our friends and families who have given us their support and encouragement. Anna, Charlie, Irene, Jerry, and William — thank you.

LINDA HART-HEWINS and JAN WELLS

Read It in the Classroom!

Organizing an Interactive Language Arts Program Grades 4~9

HEINEMANN
Portsmouth, NH

© 1992 Pembroke Publishers Limited
528 Hood Road
Markham, Ontario
L3R 3K9

Published in the U.S.A. by
Heinemann Educational Books, Inc.
361 Hanover Street
Portsmouth, NH 03801-3959
ISBN (U.S.) 0-435-08733-9

Canadian Cataloguing in Publication Data

Hart-Hewins, Linda
  Read it in the classroom

Includes bibliographical references and index.
ISBN 0-921217-75-7

1. Reading (Elementary). 2. Reading (Secondary).
I. Wells, Jan, 1948- . II. Title.

LB1573.H37 1992   372.4   C92-093086-7

Editor: David Kilgour
Design: John Zehethofer
Cover Photography: Ajay Photographics
Typesetting: Jay Tee Graphics Ltd.

Printed and bound in Canada
9 8 7 6 5 4 3 2 1

Contents

Introduction

This is an exciting time in school classrooms: teachers and students are beginning to discover what happens when we bring children's writers into the curriculum. At no other time have we had available such a wealth of reading material for children — fiction and non-fiction, trade and educational books. The constraints of using basal reading series, with their testable outcomes and in-built skills continuum, have been rejected by both publishers and educators. We know that children deserve better and thrive more on literature.

Throughout the English-speaking world, new children's bookstores are opening regularly and thousands of new titles appearing annually. Particularly in North America, Great Britain, Australia, and New Zealand, major new writers for children and young adults are emerging all the time. Parents are buying more books for their children than ever before, and in the early years more parents are reading more frequently to their children at home. There is much greater awareness of children's books and their authors than ever before.

This is also a time of growth and change for many teachers as they move away from prepackaged programs and begin to take ownership of their own classrooms. When teachers commit themselves to introducing books to children, they have to learn how to find their way through the rich array of resources to those that best suit their students and the demand of the curriculum. They have to learn how to be readers themselves; how to bring meaning to stories; how to make comparisons and judgments. When a teacher and students explore the world of children's literature together, the teacher is faced with many decisions that were previously taken care of within the structure of the basal program. Basal texts follow in order one after the other, and comprehension questions about them are written out in a workbook. All the teacher has to do is deliver the material, set the assignments, and mark the answers. Evaluation is easy because students can pass or fail based on easily measurable criteria.

When we open up the classroom to literature and allow choice within the reading program, then we need to find new ways of making book selection, new ways of finding out whether or not the students understand what they have read, and new ways of evaluating their learning.

Our first book, *Real Books for Reading*, was aimed at teachers of children ages three to eight. This book is written for teachers who want to use good books in their reading program with students ages nine to fourteen. During these six years tremendous growth and changes take place as students move from childhood to adolescence. We have written this book to help teachers understand the developing needs of this age group. We make suggestions about the organization of the classroom, the timetable, and the sorts of reading and writing activities that allow students to grow as readers. And we offer practical suggestions to teachers to help them organize a manageable and effective reading program that allows for individual differences and for the integration of various curriculum areas. Finally, in the bibliographies, we list dozens of books you can use in your classroom for all kinds of purposes.

While writing this book we have read hundreds of children's books, talked to many young readers and teachers, and engaged in endless discussions ourselves about books, organizational ideas, response activities, and evaluation techniques. We are more than ever aware that there is no one right way to run a reading or writing program, no formula that works for everyone. The worst enemy of creative teaching is orthodoxy. The best teaching is responsive, achieved by trying and responding to ideas and outcomes as they emerge. We try something and review it. Did it work? How could we do it better next time? The reflective practitioner learns constantly from his or her students. When we think we know how to do our jobs perfectly, that's when we should probably look for another career! Teaching and learning are dynamic processes and what we teach is changing all the time.

One of the issues we explore in this book is the crowded curriculum, with the many demands it makes upon students' and teachers' time — computer studies, media literacy, environmental awareness, and health education are just a few new issues that have found their way into the school program. We suggest one way to organize the reading and writing activities within the curriculum. We know it is not the only way and we hope that everyone who reads this book will take the ideas, adapt them, change them, and make them their own.

1   Getting Ready

Knowing the Learner

> So I don't want to hear about "the child," that mythical monster whom we are all supposed to have in mind when we write. I only have in mind myself and all my fifth-grade colleagues from Selby Smallwood who was retarded, to Marcia Ellison, my air-headed best friend, to Larry Jones who died of leukemia, to Donald Crawley, the class jock, who threw up at the blackboard and destroyed his image, to Georgie Bach who loved me, to Ruth Upton who didn't. We were not "the child" — we were people. Separate, distinct, with different dreams and different sorrows.[1]

Before we can design a program or construct a curriculum we must learn about our students and try to know them. Who are our students? What are their likes and dislikes, what skills do they possess, and how do they learn best? We must try to understand the sequence of language learning as a developmental process and be able to make judgments about students based on their strengths and needs. We must recognize, like Natalie Babbitt, that each young reader in our care is an individual.

We would like to introduce you to some of the children we have met. They are eleven- and twelve-year-olds from a school in a downtown neighborhood, a cosmopolitan, vibrant community with Greek stores and restaurants, Italian bakeries, a large health food supermarket, and several interesting bookstores. Some children live in homes on tree-lined streets in older buildings, many of them newly renovated, while others live above the stores and restaurants which their parents own. When they come together in the classroom they bring their varied family histories with them, but each one is very much a child of the

---

[1] Natalie Babbitt. "Remembering How It Felt" in *Indirections*, 16:1 (Ontario Council of Teachers of English, 1990), p. 62.

video and television age with a common culture as well as individual traits and customs. We asked all these children the same question: "What do you like to read?"

Dougal is the life of the classroom. He always has a quip to make and a smile on his face. He's very verbal and sometimes finds it hard to pay attention in class. When we asked him the question he replied, "I don't! I just read at school. I sort of like Matt Christopher. I really only like to read video game stuff. That's reading isn't it? Well, I do like to listen to stories. My mom reads great ones. I love *The Just So Stories*. She gets me good books to read too. I can't choose books. I don't know if I'll like them. She does though. I like joke books too."

Jonathan is a highly articulate student with an opinion on every topic. He loves to read and does so in his free time. He said, "It depends on the mood I'm in. I never just have one book at a time. I'm really into some of my dad's books at the moment. I'm just reading all the books by Tom Clancy. I think I'm into spy adventures now. Before I was into time travel. I really loved Lloyd Alexander's *Book of Three* and *The Black Cauldron*."

Sabina is a quiet student who never offers an opinion in class, prefers to work alone rather than with a partner, and seems to do only what is required by her teacher. She speaks Portuguese at home, and goes to Portuguese classes after school and on Saturdays. When asked the question she replied, "I don't know!" It took some time before she would show us what she was reading. From her desk she produced Judith Kerr's *When Hitler Stole Pink Rabbit*, Robin Muller's *Molly Whuppie and the Giant*, and *The Daring Game* by Kit Pearson. She was also reading two different Portuguese novels. When finally she began to talk to us she said, "I never read only one book at a time. I like to hop around, from Portuguese to English, hard and easy. It just depends how I feel."

Mei-Ling has just arrived in the class from China. She speaks no English and sits watching everything that goes on in the classroom. It was only after talking with her Heritage Language teacher that we discovered that Mei-Ling is an excellent reader in Chinese. She reads a wide range of novels, some more difficult than those her friends were reading.

Adrian is the hero of the boys in the class. What he does or says is often imitated by others. He spends much of his time chatting with friends. When asked, "What do you like to read?" he replied, "Nothing. I never read unless I have to and then I read magazines about cars or animals. I don't know why you have to read. My dad doesn't and he's got a job."

All the boys like Carrie. She has a wide open smile and beautiful long hair. Much of her time is spent discussing the latest fashions and talking about the boys in the class. She said, "I don't really read much. I'd rather go to a movie with my friends or watch a video. I don't mind the Judy Blume books and Sweet Valley High."

Jason is a quiet student who often seems to be in a world of his own. During group discussions he is very quiet and often refuses to answer. When asked, "What do you like to read?" he replied, "Nothing. I go to Reading Centre. I can't read unless the teacher helps me. I like to listen to stories, especially ones about animals. I can sort of read easy stuff, but I only read at Reading Centre. I never read in class."

Oliver goes nowhere without a book. In school his greatest pleasure is to read, and he spends long hours at home in his bedroom with the book of the moment. Teachers have been known to take his book away so that he will get on with other work. When asked the question he replied, "I like anything really. I don't know if I'll like a book until I read it but I'll try most things. My favorite authors are Tolkien and Isaac Asimov."

These children are just a few from one grade six classroom. Their talents and their tastes are already remarkable. Some teachers might see all this diversity as confusing, and it is! But it is also the most exciting thing about teaching. If we can work with the strengths, go with the needs, and celebrate the individual achievements of our students, we can work towards our goal of creating a true community of learners. We recognize that all of us, children included, have our personal tastes in reading. Some people read for pleasure and others do not. Some people enjoy reading about people's lives, history, and current events, while others choose romances or mysteries, spy stories or adventures. Some books are work, some are purely entertainment. Some books we read to find out more about life, and some we read to escape from it. At different times and for different purposes we read for information — technical manuals, instructions, and professional reading material. All this reading requires different sorts of skills; in order to make sense of the printed word, the reader must have a purpose and a context for the reading as well as the ability to decode. Whatever our abilities as readers, the act of reading is essentially idiosyncratic. We make meaning in the light of our own personal experiences; what we bring to the reading is as important as what is on the page.

Young people between the ages of nine and fourteen are exciting, volatile, and affectionate, with fierce loyalties and passionate convictions. They also undergo tremendous changes during these years. Our goal for these students is simple. We want to convince them that reading books is a good way to spend their time. We want to hook them on books, and research has shown that these are the vital years for fostering the habit. If we lose children at this stage, we may have lost them forever. We want to help Sabina and Carrie and Jason to find reasons for becoming readers. Many children learn to read, but not all learn that reading is a resource for life, a source of pleasure, recreation, and personal satisfaction, as well as a vital resource in all other learning.

Primary-age children are desperate to learn to read. They struggle away until the magical day when finally the squiggles begin to make sense to them. When that happens, they have mastered the basic skills of decoding print, but this is only the beginning of a lifelong learning process, for none of us can ever say that we have mastered all there is to know about reading and writing. The learning becomes a question of what we *do* with the ability to read and write, what use we make of it. We go on developing our knowledge and our ability as readers and writers by applying our skills in written language for increasingly challenging and complex purposes. We develop habits of reading and writing that form the patterns of our adult lives as literate human beings. How can teachers keep alive the enthusiasm of the fledgling reader so that reading becomes a lifelong pleasure?

When we read, we enter what Tolkien has called the secondary world, where the time and place of the real world would give way to the time and place of the imaginary world of the book.[2] Nine-year-olds have, in most cases, just learned how to

---

[2] J.R.R. Tolkien. "On Fairy Stories" in *Tree and Leaf* (Allen Unwin, 1964), p. 36.

read fluently and are remarkably well disposed to enter the secondary world. At this age children live for large portions of their waking hours in the world of their imaginations. This is the age at which extended play scenarios can continue over weeks and months. A friend recently confided that at the age of ten he spent one whole summer in Montreal with a gang of boys (no girls were included) playing "Monkey World". As King of the Monkey World he led a rule-governed populace through a series of imaginary escapades. Props were few and far between, but conflicts arose and were resolved within the laws of the kingdom. Young children enter the secondary world of books with the same suspension of reality. They can easily become "lost in a book". Through imagination they conjure up images of scenes, people, and actions. Given the limited life experience of the nine-year-old, the imagination must surely supply more of this imagery than it does for the adult reader who can draw upon a larger memory bank. Yet children have no difficulty visualizing Middle Earth or Terabithia. The world of children's books is a world with no boundaries, where anything can happen and often does. Talking animals, streams which offer immortality to those who drink from them, princesses who outwit dragons, and pebbles that can grant wishes are all part of the secondary world. When a book is too difficult for a young reader, it is perhaps because there is not enough in the text to match with personal experience to allow the imagination to work and meaning to be made. The best writers for children use words with enough clarity that visual pictures can float into the mind. In choosing books for young readers, this is a quality to be considered carefully. We believe that the choice of books in our program is key to the nurturing of the love of reading. We must cater to all diverse tastes and disparate skills of our students until the reading habit is firmly established and they have learned to love reading.

As they grow from childhood to early adolescence, students become more volatile, throwing themselves into projects with unremitting enthusiasm, or else refusing to cooperate — with equal vehemence. They begin to define their own views of themselves, to create their own identities. The pressure of belonging and finding approval within a group become increasingly important to them, and social behavior, the way they dress and talk, and the things they believe in are often determined by their peer group. They become passionately interested in social issues and concerned about their rights and the rights of others. They can be a tough challenge to teachers, but the rewards of working with this age group are enormous.

Organizing the Environment for Learning

The cornerstone of our program is the classroom climate. We have to establish an atmosphere of respect in which everyone's efforts are valued and in which work is honored. We expect cooperation, collaboration, and care, and we talk about what these words mean. In a program founded on the intrinsic worth of each individual there are responsibilities as well as rights. Establishing the norms of classroom behavior is important and we expect our students to care about their own learning and about each other. Modelling what we expect of them is our main strategy.

We talk to students in ways in which we expect them to talk to us and to each other — openly, honestly, and respectfully. Our interactions with students are designed to enhance learning, so in talking about books we try to ask open-ended questions that allow the students to tell us their thoughts and feelings. We ask them to share with us the pictures in their imaginations. We do not test them on their comprehension by using predetermined questions with "right" answers. Ten-year-old William, an avid reader forever lost in a book at home, was asked, "What is the worst thing about school?" Without missing a beat he replied, "Comprehension. It makes reading so boring."

The ways in which we organize the learning environment are also important. For individual writing activities students need privacy and quiet. Positioning carrels at the side of the classroom, facing the walls, can be one way to provide this atmosphere. Most classrooms have a desk or seat at a table for each individual, and frequently there is some student ownership of this particular space. This is where the students sit to do their work, and they may store their possessions in the desk. In such a classroom arrangement it is important to provide the following areas:

- a classroom library display space, where books are housed and displayed attractively. Students go there to choose and exchange books, but return to their seats to read.
- a meeting place for the whole class. If we want students to listen attentively to something read aloud then we must have a

gathering place where all can be comfortable and close to the reader. Young children have no problem sitting on the floor, but as they get older they tend not to use the floor as working space. We feel that teenagers are comfortable stretched out on the floor or curled up on floor cushions, so we have a home base with carpet and cushions where the group can sit together when necessary. This space is used during the work period by students who wish to spread work out on the floor, or to read privately. One teacher we know built a tree-house in her classroom, and another constructed a "Hobbit Hole". The students can help design and build imaginative environments in which reading or conversations between two or three people can take place quietly.

- a space in which small group interaction can take place. A large table or grouping of desks makes a good meeting place for the Reading Circle. Writing conferences can also take place around this table or grouping.

- storage areas where art materials are kept. Students should be independent in finding the supplies they need and returning to their desks with them.

If the students are agreeable, a far more flexible room arrangement allows for more possibilities in terms of art projects, filmmaking, drama, and so on. Each person must be provided with private storage space somewhere but need not retain ownership of any particular space. Then desks and tables can be arranged to create centres — places where certain things happen. At one centre, for instance, dictionaries and editing tools may be provided, and students take their writing there to use those resources. At another centre there can be art materials — paper, paints, found materials, glue, scissors, etc. At this centre the students make artefacts to accompany their written work. At another centre the classroom library can be housed and books displayed. Picture books look good if they are arranged with the covers facing out. Places to sit comfortably can make this an attractive place to work.

This kind of room arrangement allows for more movement and creates fewer problems with supplies. Students must work cooperatively and learn to share materials. Allowing students the opportunity to move around is important — this is an age at which many find it physically uncomfortable to sit still for long.

However we arrange the furniture, we believe it should be in consultation with the students. This is their working environment as well as ours, and if we want them to share the responsibility of keeping it tidy, using it respectfully, and caring about its success as a place in which to work, then the least we can do is consult them about their needs.

Choosing Books

So what sorts of books do we use and how do we select them? One of our fundamental beliefs in teaching young readers is that they need choice in the reading program. We must respect their differing styles and tastes, needs and passions, and offer as much opportunity for individual decision-making as possible. Remembering that Dougal and Sabina and Jonathan and Adrian all share our classroom, we must provide a wide range of books from which they may choose their individual reading material. This does not mean that all the students never read the same book. Nor does it mean that they pursue totally individual programs. There are times when everyone listens to the same book read aloud. There are times when certain reading is prescribed for a specific purpose. During the course of a year we provide a balance between individual choice and guided selection as we try to lead the students towards more challenging books.

At the end of this book you will find bibliographies of books that students have read and to which they have responded in talk, in art, and in writing. These bibliographies are organized by theme. In every case there is some aspect of each book that relates to the "big idea" under consideration, but this does not mean that each book belongs exclusively to one category. Most good books have many layers of meaning, and one of our goals is to help students to find the most important thing about a book for them — a personal meaning that gives the book a real significance for their lives. *Charlotte's Web* is at one and the same time a book about friendship and loyalty, about spiders and pigs, about growing up on a farm and the end of childhood, about life and death. To try to categorize it is impossible. Yet in order to help children to make connections, to see possibilities and alternatives, it is sometimes useful to have everyone read books that are in some way related to each other, by style, by subject matter, or by theme.

Our bibliographies are starting points and you will want to add your own titles depending on what you have available. You should start any work with children's literature by exploring your school library. You will also likely want to visit the public library and make time to talk to experienced childrens' librarians about books. Once you are hooked, you will find yourself, like us, subscribing to reviewing journals and reading books about children's books. You will visit local bookstores where there are more enthusiasts and experts with whom to share your passion. You will begin to hunt down children's authors, frequenting their sessions at conferences and inviting them to your school. You will become a teacher who knows that creating a literate classroom for your students involves you as a reader.

Our bibliographies reflect our concern for good literature, but they also take into account the fact that many young readers in our classrooms need books with good stories in them that will provide a bridge to more difficult reading. Ultimately, we want all our students to read the very best of literature, by writers like Katherine Paterson, William Mayne, Russell Hoban, and Philippa Pearce, whose work challenges and enriches. No one could make the case for good literature better than Katherine Paterson. In *The Gates of Excellence* she writes,

> There are countless [others] — really good books. Good or even
> great because they make the right connections. They pull
> together for us a world that is falling apart. They are the words
> that integrate us, stretch us, comfort us and heal us. They are
> the words that mirror the Word of creation, bringing order out
> of chaos.[3]

Books are not to be prescribed like medicine to make students better people, or even to improve their reading skills (though of course they will do that); they are encounters with ideas that somehow leave readers transformed. A good book should leave us thinking or feeling differently than we did before we read it. As we select books for the classroom, we bear this in mind, as well as the wide range of students' abilities.

---

[3] Katherine Paterson. "Words", in *The Gates of Excellence: On Reading and Writing Books for Children* (E.P. Dutton, 1981), p. 18.

2 The Components of a Literature-Based Reading Program

You're convinced! You have decided to abandon your basal readers and expand your reading program to include more literature. You have selected books to meet the reading abilities, ages, interests, and tastes of your students, as well as meeting curriculum requirements. You have displayed the books attractively in the room, and both you and the students are enthusiastic and anxious to get started. But where do you go from here? What are the ingredients of a literature-based reading program? What do you need to do every day? What should be accomplished in a week or during the course of one unit or term? What are the essential components of a good reading program?

Reading Aloud

> I read with my students. I show them what I'm reading and I talk about and lend my books. I tell them reading is a habit, one that shaped my life and it has so much meaning I don't know if I could go on living if I suddenly couldn't read.[1]

The first component is the **daily** read-aloud time, when the teacher shares literature with the class. We suggest that you read aloud at least twice a day to your students. Reading first thing in the morning sets a positive tone for the day. It brings the group together to focus, to think, and to share as a community of learners. Reading last thing in the afternoon ends the day on a note that consolidates and nurtures that sense of community. One of the most important reasons for reading aloud is the development of trust and belonging within the group. David Booth and Bob Barton write:

---

[1] Nancie Atwell. *In the Middle: Writing, Reading and Learning with Adolescents* (Heinemann, 1987), p. 48.

When children become a community of listeners, they lay aside their own egocentricity, and become a tribe.[2]

The common laughter and tears we often share as we are moved by literature creates a sense of belonging. In this atmosphere students are more likely to take risks, to express opinions and feelings. Learning to respect each other's opinions and feelings and to be sensitive listeners is part of sharing literature.

What Do We Read?

We choose from a wide variety of resources — fiction and non-fiction, poetry and prose. We share picture books, poetry, novels, short stories, magazine articles, and the students' own writing. We read what *we* like, and we are not afraid to stop if the story is not going well and to discuss why the story is not sucessful. Non-fiction material is an especially important component as we move towards an integration of language arts and other curriculum areas.

Many Kinds of Writing

The read-aloud time enables teachers to share many different kinds of writing, some of it too difficult for the students to read independently. The books we share in the read-aloud are usually ones that are harder to read than the students' independent reading level. Thus a grade five class can become absorbed in Leon Garfield's *Smith*, which has rich language and an eighteenth-century setting. The sound of the words is the sound of British literary language, distanced by time and place from the rhythms of twentieth-century North American children's voices. Through our reading, the class can share in Smith's life, feel afraid for him, feel angry that he is unjustly thrown into Newgate prison, and share in his triumphant vindication as the plot is resolved. There is no need to explain all the unfamiliar words; the context of the story carries us along and the children learn to fill in the blanks with their own understandings. Sometimes we may stop and make sure that a difficult but important word has been understood, but usually we let the writer's voice carry on uninterrupted.

---

[2] Bob Barton and David Booth. *Stories in the Classroom: Storytelling, Reading Aloud, and Roleplaying with Children* (Pembroke, 1990), p. 31.

Two kinds of read-aloud books which are often overlooked in classes for children ages nine and up are poetry and picture books. It's worth examining their use here.

Poetry

Poetry is also a feature of our daily read-aloud time. We don't dissect poetry but enjoy its rhythm, sounds, and cadences. Discussion may follow if the students respond spontaneously, but that is not our first concern.

We hope that once we hook students on the possibilities of poetry by introducing them to a steady diet of many forms, they will eventually begin to read and write poetry for themselves. They will gradually come to understand that a poem can encapsulate thoughts and feelings. To paraphrase Bill Moore, in poetry the words mean more than the words mean. If we spend too long looking for the "hidden meanings" we may spoil the magic. Somehow children lose that first spontaneous love of word-play that characterizes playground chants and skipping rhymes. We want to keep that enchantment with the magic of words alive. We agree with Bill Moore and David Booth when they say:

> All children can benefit from poetry — the pre-school child who claps along, the gifted reader who seeks out the most sophisticated poets, the reluctant reader who finds that short, sharp poems taste delicious, the child new to English, who finds the rhythms and the rhymes memorable, the young adult who finds his or her feelings reflected in the words.[3]

Some of the most effective poetry to read aloud is narrative verse such as *The Cremation of Sam McGee* and *The Highwayman*. We love the variety that poetry offers through its many styles and forms. Like picture books, poems can be powerful vehicles for engaging the imagination, without the time required to work with longer fiction. We have included in our bibliographies a list of poetry books from which we love to read aloud and which have been enjoyed by our students.

Picture Books

Picture books are very important to us in our work with older children. Contrary to popular belief picture books are not just

---

[3] David Booth and Bill Moore. *Poems Please! Sharing Poetry with Children* (Pembroke, 1988), p. 37.

for babies! There are many very sophisticated picture books with layers of meaning in both words and pictures. The pictures hold the eye while the words weave into the imagination.

Taken together, words and pictures produce meanings beyond their individual images. One of our favorite picture books is *John Brown, Rose and the Midnight Cat* by Jenny Wagner. It is more than a story about a dog who scares away a cat. It confronts the reader with loneliness, the nature of friendship, and the pain that jealousy can cause. As we see John Brown curled up in deep contemplation with one paw on Rose's slipper, we read:

John Brown thought. He thought all through lunch time and when supper time came, he was still thinking.[4]

As we look at the accompanying picture it takes us into those thoughts, into John Brown's feelings. We know that he is reconsidering his actions in driving away the Midnight Cat because of the hurt it has caused his friend.

Books like this can stimulate wide-ranging discussion, thoughtful writing, and imaginative responses. In our bibliographies we have included picture books as well as novels as we believe them to be an important literary form for young adolescents. A picture book is a microcosm of a novel. It has structure, form, plot, character, and setting, and yet it can be read in one sitting. A picture book can be enjoyed and discussed and can then provide stimulus for the students' own work.

Furthermore, a book with a short text and the visual clues provided by pictures can be an invaluable resource for students who are just becoming confident as independent readers. The support of pictures in helping those experiencing difficulty in learning to read, or those who are learning to read in English as a second language, is often underestimated. We need to give the picture books in our classroom a validity that is sometimes overlooked as students move into the reading of novels.

Picture books provide us with opportunities to work orally with the whole class in response to a story. Through discussions we demonstrate the sorts of things we want the students to notice when they are reading. This is a time when they can develop their skills in prediction and critical thinking and in responding to text. They learn how to defend their opinions by reference

---

[4] Jenny Wagner. *John Brown, Rose and the Midnight Cat* (Puffin, 1977).

to the work — both words and pictures — how to listen to each other, and how to ask relevant questions. Talking about texts is one of the most important things that we do in the classroom, and we shall return to it later.

Reading for Enjoyment

We read aloud with a sense of enjoyment. Sometimes we practise reading to ourselves beforehand: it is important that the way we read aloud is interesting and sensitive to the meaning of the material. There's nothing more soporific on a hot afternoon than the droning voice of a teacher reading in a monotone. Our voice must be expressive and communicate our sense of why this piece is worth reading, because our most important reason for reading aloud is the sharing of enjoyment. We know that when we read aloud we have the opportunity to introduce our students to wonderful stories and to further hook them on the act of reading. By sharing our enthusiasm we hope to instill in them a love of books. We believe that we must model a love of reading if we want students to become readers too.

Shared Responses

Reading aloud can calm a class that is restless or stressed. Timetable constraints should not prevent us from reading aloud whenever we judge it to be an appropriate moment. However, reading aloud at the beginning of a period of language activities has a very specific purpose. It offers the teacher the opportunity to use the shared text in any number of ways related to the work that the students will do later. It allows for demonstration and modelling.

The read-aloud time is a catalyst for thinking. It provides ideas for the class to discuss. The sorts of responses we can make to literature can be explored using a common text with which the whole class is engaged. If students work together to explore one text then they become familiar with ways of thinking, talking, and writing about books which they can then use in their independent and small group work. We can use the shared text to demonstrate the activities we want the students to try. If we want them to write in response journals, or make diagrams which explore relationships between characters, or draw maps of the setting of a story, or write a sequel or an alternative ending, we must *demonstrate* our expectations before we send them off to try these things independently.

We think this demonstration and time spent working as a whole class are important components of a literature-based program, because our ultimate goal is to enable students to choose from a range of responses the one that best suits the understandings they have found in a book. They will eventually show us what they have understood in their independent reading through the responses they make. Before they can make these responses individually, however, they need time to explore them with others, using a common text.

When we read aloud we show students that we care about books. We create an environment where the sort of "literary gossip" that Nancie Atwell describes can take place. We recommend books to each other, tell how they make us feel, and talk about the memories they provoke. We make comparisons and share enthusiasms. This is the cornerstone of our whole program, and we cannot teach children to be readers and writers without it!

Individual Private Reading Time

> An important part of the learning cycle is the opportunity for the learner to play around with or put into effect the hypotheses he's currently working on.[5]

We learn to read by reading. Time to practise is a critical component of all new learning. We need time to use the skill we are developing. Daily reading time when everyone reads privately is part of a successful literature-based program. It's a time for each student to be lost in a book.

This time can be at the beginning of the afternoon, after recess, or in those odd moments that occur in a timetable when students are waiting for "the next thing" to happen. The length of time spent varies with the age of the students, but fifteen minutes a day is a good start.

What Do They Read?

During private reading time we offer a choice and do not prescribe reading. The students are free to select any book, magazine,

---

[5] Brian Cambourne. *The Whole Story: Natural Learning and the Acquisition of Literacy in the Classroom* (Ashton Scholastic, 1988), p. 70.

or article they wish from the classroom collection. Some students take this opportunity to continue to read the book they are currently reading in their language arts class, others do not. As time goes by, however, more and more of the students do choose to use this time to read the book from their language time. If this time is to be worthwhile and productive, the materials selected must reflect the age and ever-changing interests of the class. There must be materials that span many reading levels so that the needs of all the readers in the class will be met. We include picture books and magazines, as we find that this kind of material is often attractive to our reluctant readers. At times even our most able readers enjoy these materials. Before making any selections for our classroom library we always survey the class to find out what they like to read and who their favorite authors are. Extensive use of the school library is critical. Its rich supply of materials allows us to keep our classroom libraries fresh. It enables us to borrow specific materials that will link private reading time to current topics of interest or themes that we are studying. Thus we plan ahead with our teacher-librarian what we will borrow as we move from theme to theme throughout the school year.

Teachers Read Too

We demonstrate that we value recreational reading — reading for pleasure — not only by timetabling for this activity but also by reading ourselves. During our private reading time everyone reads silently — including us. At first it was difficult to resist the temptation to take a few minutes to do other things, such as holding individual reading conferences, but when we were able to resist this temptation we found that the whole group became more focused. When we read we are showing again by example that reading is important to us. This time also gives us a few moments to catch up on some of the literature our students are reading so that we are able to respond in an informed manner to their thoughts and reflections. We find that the books we choose to read often inspire some of our more reluctant readers to try something more challenging. The single greatest motivation for students to read a book is a personal recommendation by their teacher.

Keeping a Log

All the reading done during private reading time, and at other times too, should be recorded by each student in a reading log. This booklet is kept in the student's work portfolio. It is a valuable document, allowing us to see at a glance:

- what the students are reading;
- how long it takes them to read something;
- what their reading preferences are;
- where the reading takes place.

In reading conferences, as we talk about their logs with the students, we can

- make suggestions about books they might enjoy next and record these suggestions;
- nudge them towards books that will challenge them more;
- involve them in self-evaluation as they set goals for themselves;
- keep records of comments made about books.

The advantage of this type of comprehensive record-keeping is that it involves the students in self-evaluation and also keeps anecdotal comments positive and useful. It allows us to nudge the learning. Here is an example of a page from a log book kept by Sabina.

Reading Log

Title	Date	Reader	Comment
The Stone-Faced Boy	Oct 14	Sabina	pg 15 I hate the Bus driver
"	Oct 15	Sabina	pg 35 ☺ great
Eating the Alphabet	Oct 15	Sabina & George	Fun
The Stone Faced Boy	Oct 16	Readers' Circle	Sabina re-told the story with clarity ML.
"	Oct 16	Sabina	pg 71 – exciting
"	Oct 17	Sabina	pg 92 I can't wait to finish
"	Oct 18	Sabina	FINISHED good book
Angel Child/ Dragon Child	Oct 21	Sabina	sad
"	Oct 22	Sabina	I like the ending
The Jolly Postman	Oct 22	Sabina & George	we liked the letters
Angel Child/ Dragon Child	Oct 23	Readers' Circle	offered a link to their own life MH.
The Trail of the Screaming Teenager	Oct 23	Sabina	pg 42 – easy
"	Oct 24	Sabina	A funny book

Title	Date	Reader	Comment
Journey to Jo'burg	Oct 25	Sabina & Mrs K	Suggested Journey to Jo'Burg to Mrs K.
"	Oct 25	Sabina	sad beginning pg 17
"	Oct 28	Sabina	a scarey book pg 41
Things I like	Oct 29	Sabina & George	George read this good reading
Journey to Jo'burg	Oct 29	Sabina	pg 60 - sad
"	Oct 30	Sabina	finished - a thinking book
	Oct 30	Readers' Circle	re-tells well decided to offer a book review.
Hairy Tales and Nursery Crimes	Nov 4	Sabina	I need a funny book
	Nov 5	Sabina	great!
Rainbow Goblins	Nov 5	Sabina & George	We loved the pictures

George is Sabina's six-year-old buddy reader.

Such logs measure the quantity of the students' reading. They also show us the range and quality of the literature that is being enjoyed. One way of drawing the students' attention to these things is to have them keep a graph which charts the types of material they read. In the following example the students color in a square every time they read something.

What did you read?   Each time you finish a title, record the date in the appropriate square.

Your name	Allison							
poetry								
picture book	Sept 10	Sept 11						
fairy tale	Sept 12							
folktale or legend								
NOVELS: adventure	Sept 16							
fantasy	Oct 9							
historical								
humourous								
family story	Sept 25							
animal story								
time travel								
science fiction								
other mystery	Oct 29	Nov 6.						
NON-FICTION magazines	Oct 1	Oct 4						
jokes and riddles	Oct 19							
information books								
other								

Time to Respond to Reading

Comprehension of a text requires that the reader recreate its meaning, constructing in the light of his or her experience the author's intended meaning. We believe, with Louise Rosenblatt, that reading is a transaction, a bringing to and taking meaning from the written text.[6]

---

[6] Ralph Peterson and Maryann Eeds. *Grand Conversations: Literature Groups in Action* (Scholastic Bright Ideas, 1990), p. 12.

Reading aloud and providing time for the students to just read on their own are the first two components of a literature-based reading program. On their own, however, they are not enough. There is a third vital component, reading that is done with a deeper consciousness, reading that is contemplated, discussed, and shared with others. Through *response activities* our students come to make sense of what they have read and to make links from the world of books to the experiences of their own lives. They gain deeper insights into the meanings that lie behind authors' words. They gain understandings of how books work to change our lives.

We provide for this meaning-centred reading by expecting the students to read books that will give them something important to think about and by structuring opportunities for them to respond to this reading in many different ways. In our language program the students engage in some sort of response activity every day.

A Wide Variety of Responses

In order for all their voices to be heard, students' responses must take a variety of forms. The nature of young adolescents is such that they respond to choice and to a variety of means of expression: we give them time to talk, to draw, to construct, to act out, and to write about the books they have read. While attempting to allow for individual differences in learning style and personal talent, we are also developing critical thinking skills. It takes careful analysis and synthesis of ideas before you can choose which type of response is the best one for you and for the book you want to share. Some books speak about people — characters and relationships. Others have a strong sense of the importance of place. Some may evoke an oral or artistic response. Others demand that we write a response, that we put our own ideas about a story or topic down on paper. Students need to be free to choose the response they see as most appropriate.

However, if we begin by offering too much choice before the forms of the various responses have been learned, the results will be chaos. This is why we suggest that at the beginning of the year the entire class work together using a book read aloud. We have learned to go slowly and to introduce response activities one at a time. By the end of the year the students will have learned how to write in a dialogue journal, how to make a literary socio-gram and construct a character profile. They will have at their fingertips many strategies for retelling stories. They will be used to writing sequels and thinking of alternative endings for stories. They will have worked individually, in pairs, and in small groups designing posters and making short video and slide presentations to "sell" their favorite books to their peers. Mapping the journeys of main characters and writing in role are other strategies with which our students will have become familiar. And, of course, they will have learned to think and to talk about the stories they have read.

How Often Do They Respond?

There simply isn't enough time to ask students to respond formally with a written response to all the books they have read. We suggest they make at least one response a week and present it in a Reading Circle. They may select the form of the response as long as they show that over time they are varying the ways in which they tell others about their books. To ensure that they do vary their choices a tracking sheet like the one below can be used.

Responses that can be used to demonstrate an understanding of books read	
Response	**Date used**
Response journal entry	
New book cover.	
Book review	
Poster for book	
Character profile	
Retell story from one character's point of view	

Reading Circles

> I don't know what I think about a book until we've talked about it. — Sarah, age 8.[7]

The Reading Circle is a place in which small groups of students come together to share their books. It is the most vital and important part of the reading classroom, for it is here that the students practise their skills in "booktalk". Once a week all our students have the opportunity to meet in a small group with us to talk about their reading. We timetable one group of six to eight students a day to come to the Reading Circle. (The other students are engaged in their independent response activities at this time.) These meetings may not be too long, as the teacher also needs to hold individual short conferences with everyone in the class. Much booktalk that goes on in the room is unplanned and spontaneous, but this is a *planned* opportunity for everyone to come to the group and talk about their current work. The focus of the work done in these groups is not always the same: as theme studies develop and response activities are learned, the conversation will take a very different form. Initially, however, this is an exploration of books through talk.

Who Takes Part in Reading Circles?

We believe that Reading Circles should be composed of students of all abilities. Less articulate children learn in the company of those who are more verbal. Many students who don't write with confidence will be well able to talk about the ideas and beliefs contained in books. The readability levels of the books shared may vary, but all the books we choose for inclusion in the program will have something of interest for us to discuss, some issues for us to sink our teeth into.

When we have students who are proficient readers in a first language other than English we try to include, whenever possible, books that they can read in that language. We have found that many of those students who are learning English as a second language can speak and understand much more than they can read and write. Reading first-language materials enables these students to participate in Reading Circles.

---

[7] Aidan Chambers. *Booktalk* (The Bodley Head, 1985), p. 106.

Sharing What We Read

What do we talk about in the Reading Circle? We come together to share our perceptions and to extend our thinking. Sometimes everyone has read the same book. Sometimes the group shares a number of titles. Whatever the case, if genuine responses to literature are to be made, there must be an open-ended dialogue which respects the opinions of all the members of the group. The teacher is as much a learner as the students here, and no one has the "right" answers.

The teacher's questions and comments set the tone and must therefore be chosen carefully. This does not mean that there are right or wrong questions for circles, but it does mean that we have to try to deepen the students' level of thinking with our questions and the feedback we give them. The following starters have proved useful in encouraging students to move from descriptive talk, through personal associations and memories, to a deeper understanding of the meanings of texts. We begin by choosing *one* opening remark that will be open-ended enough to allow the students to give us their first impressions without fear of being judged. As Aidan Chambers says, the most effective invitation is, "Tell me about your book." The first response that readers make is always descriptive, and the students will automatically begin to retell the story. One of the skills that has to be developed is that of synthesis. The whole group can't listen to a blow by blow account of the plot, but we do need to know the main events, and so the students have to learn to keep their descriptions to the point.

Describing the Text

We begin with a simple retelling, a description of the text. This establishes what we are talking about. It gives all the members of the group a starting point for discussion, such as:

- Tell us about your book.
- If you haven't finished the story, what do you think is going to happen?
- Tell us what you noticed in the story.
- Was there anything you didn't understand?
- What do you like about the book?

Making Personal Connections

Depending upon the sort of dialogue that is emerging we try to ask further questions that will move the conversation onwards to consider associations and connections. By analogy to their own experiences children can consider the actions of characters in books:

- Tell us how this story reminds you of your own life.
- Tell us what thoughts/ideas this story evokes.
- Who do you know that is like the character in the book?
- Where have you been that reminds you of a place in the book?
- What do you think you would have done in this situation?
- How do you feel about that?

Looking for Patterns and Significance

Having explored the students' personal connection we might want to consider the significance of the writing for us as readers. What did it mean to us? What do we think it was saying? What motivations did the characters have? What tensions and moods did the writer create that affected us as we read?

- Which part of the book was the most successful, from your point of view?
- What do you think this book is really all about?
- Why do you think the author bothered to write this book?
- Where do you agree/disagree with what the writer is saying?
- What do you think should be done about the sort of problem described in the book?
- Do you know any other books by this author?
- Tell me about some other books you know that are like this one.

The questions we ask depend entirely on the flow of the conversation. As the students become more experienced and confident it should become possible to hand more and more of the dialogue over to them. They will begin to ask relevant questions, to ask each other for more details, clarifications, and personal reactions.

We try to impress upon our students that in a successful discussion the participants must be able to justify their remarks and opinions with reference to the text. Sometimes we ask the students to find the particular place to which they are referring and to read out a short passage. To help prepare them for this exercise we suggest that as they are reading silently they watch for interesting passages they might like to share in the Reading Circle. Post-It notes are available for them to mark the parts that interest them.

Exploring Genres

Later in the year the focus of the Reading Circle can change. Now the groups may meet to explore a particular literary genre, such as mystery, fantasy, realistic or "problem" novels, science fiction, or picture books. There are issues to be discussed that relate to what happens in these types of books. With the students we can explore the common features that run through all the books they have read. We need to ask questions that help the students see literary patterns. It is important to emphasize that this sort of discussion happens most successfully later in the year after the students have had lots of open-ended discussions about a wide range of stories from different genres.

As an example, here are some questions that can be used if all the students in the group have read a fairy tale or folktale. In the Reading Circle the students compare the individual stories that they have read and begin to uncover formulas and structures that are present in folktales from around the world.

- Tell us who the main characters in the story are.
- How would you classify each of these characters (hero/heroine, villain, victim)?
- Tell us about the main problem in the story.
- Who fixes the problem? Describe this character.
- Who is made to suffer in your story? What is this character like?
- Who causes suffering in your story? Describe this character.

The Teacher's Role

Our role in these small group discussions is critical. We need to do more than just facilitate the conversation with carefully chosen questions. We also need to ensure that all the members of the group are given a chance to speak and that others listen carefully. We have to be aware that some students will respond more readily than others and that we need strategies to draw all members of the Reading Circle into the discussion. We model and reinforce the expectation that everyone should give attention to the person speaking. We invite each person to contribute by using such remarks as, "I'd like to hear what you think of that. . ." or, "Would you respond to that, please?" This strategy keeps everyone focused and practising good listening skills as well as ensuring that everyone gets a turn to speak. We also demonstrate ways of talking and thinking about books by the contributions we make to the conversation. By offering our thoughts and opinions we can provide a springboard for discussion. A comment such as "I really liked the part when. . ." can start the ball rolling.

We also use the time spent in the Reading Circle to carry out diagnostic and formative evaluation. We record our observations systematically. A note pad kept by our side is useful for making quick jottings that can be referred to later. Any significant observations are transferred to a more permanent record-keeping system. We build up a student profile based upon these classroom observations, made at regular intervals throughout the year. One of the best ways to observe a student's understandings is to record short snippets of actual speech. Jot down what the student says and reflect on it later. Once in a while it is interesting to make a tape recording of a Reading Circle in action and replay it to yourself at your leisure. This practice offers insights into the thinking and involvement of the students in the dialogue. It also helps you evaluate the facilitating nature of your questions and comments.

Using the Library or Resource Centre

The library is an extension of the classroom. It houses a wide array of print and non-print materials to which students have access for borrowing and researching. Without the resources of a well-stocked library it is very difficult to run a strong literature-based program. The students must be able to select material from a wide range of resources to extend and complement the books that are housed in their classroom collection.

We deliberately structure some of the reading response activities so that the students are required to use the library. We try to build in opportunities for them to learn the mechanics of library use as they explore the issues in the books they are reading. Through activities such as finding other works by particular authors or illustrators, researching biographical information about authors and illustrators, or finding different versions of a fairy

tale, the students learn how to use the card or computer cata-
logue, how to use an encyclopedia, and how to take concise and
useful point-form notes. Sometimes the students undertake
research projects, together with the teacher-librarian, on places,
people, and events they encounter in their reading. Thus library
and research skills are learned in the context of exploring
literature.

Teacher-librarians are knowledgeable professionals who can
help the students find their way around the library and use it
effectively; they are also a source of information and knowledge
about the books the students are reading. We teach our students
to turn to the librarian for help in extending and clarifying their
understandings about the books they are reading. We view
teacher-librarians as partners in both the delivery of a literature-
based program and its planning.

Booktalks

One of the most important roles played by the teacher-librarian
is to help keep the students informed about new materials and
to be enthusiastic about the materials in the library. This is accomplished through regular booktalks. We always begin a new theme
with a booktalk session in the library. Most book selection takes
place as a result of personal recommendation, either by friends
or by teachers. The role of teachers and librarians in whetting
the appetites of young readers is vital. The students will want
to read a book not because we say they must, but because we
have read it and recommended it with enthusiasm. Often librarians and teachers begin booktalks by saying, "This is my favorite
book of all time and I can't wait to hear what you think about
it!" The list of "all-time favorites" is constantly being revised!

The students also need help in learning how to choose a book
that is within their reading ability. Some will tend to choose books
that are too difficult for them because they are afraid of looking
less capable than other students. Others will consistently choose
material that doesn't stretch them. The principle we follow is
that of "guided choice", where there is a role for the teacher and
teacher-librarian in helping the students to find appropriate books.

Planning with the Teacher-Librarian

Because we view librarians as partners in the planning and

36

Library Schedule

Beginning Nov. 4/91

Time	Monday	Tuesday	Wednesday	Thursday	Friday
9:00-9:30	Lisa Marcon 108 Kind.	Mary Carrino 203 (Gr. 1/2) until Christmas	Walt Stepura Group (201)	Darlene Alberts 202 (Gr. 1) until Christmas	Walt Stepura Group (201)
9:35-10:10	Open	Mike Kalynowsky Group (304)	Walt Stepura Group (201)	Open	Mike Kalynowsky Group (304)
10:30-11:05	Open	Mike Kalynowsky Group (304)	Open	Open	Open
11:05-11:40	Library	Open Administration Time	Library	Open Preparation Time	Open

delivery of a literature-based reading program we schedule time to plan with them. Together we schedule the times when groups will work in the library under their supervision. Together we devise the nature of the activities. The library is a true extension of the classroom. To achieve flexibility of programming we prefer an open schedule in the library whereby the teacher-librarian is able to book periods to work with small groups on specific topics. We have found that whole class visits to the library for the exchange of books prohibit the sort of teaching partnerships that facilitate successful literature-based programs. Here is a sample library schedule for two grade five/six classes that were working on a theme of "Conflict and Changes in Children's Lives" both in their classrooms and in the library.

Buddy Reading

Any skill is developed through consistent practice. Just because they have mastered the mechanics of reading, it isn't true that students of nine and ten years of age and even older no longer need opportunities to read aloud. It is often through reading a piece aloud that we come to fully appreciate its meaning. Reading aloud also helps to develop expression and sensitivity to the meanings of particular words and to the mood of a story.

One way to provide more of this critical practice time is to start a "buddy reading" program with a younger class. Teachers of primary children know that the more good stories their children listen to, the more easily they learn to read themselves. Consequently, there is usually no problem in finding a kindergarten or grade one teacher who would like to partner her/his class with older reading buddies who will read aloud to younger students one on one.

A buddy program can take place during school hours and work most successfully when the following conditions are in place.

- Limit the sharing to two or three times a week. If you do it too often it loses its impact and disrupts other programs.
- Timetable buddy reading to take place immediately before or after recess.
- Confine the locations in which it takes place. Use the library, the two classrooms involved, and the halls, but do not allow enterprising individuals to hide in cupboards or find locations outside the building!

- Set a time limit of fifteen minutes. Many students enjoy this program so much that they will spend hours engaged in reading together. This, however, will disrupt other learning.
- Monitor the selection of materials carefully. The older students need to select material that is suitable for their listeners.
- Have both younger and older students record their reading in their individual reading logs. This means that two records, filled in at the end of each session, will be kept and contribute to the running record of all books read in all contexts during the year by each student. Together the students should decide how they felt about the story shared and record these feelings. The older student may need to help the younger student with this task. (See buddy reading card below.)

Title of book, poem read	Date read	Reader	Comment
The Inn Keepers Daughter	Sept 25	Me	Pg 13-31 The mother's character is a bit odd
"	Sept 26	Me	Pg 31-43 Boring
I	Sept 26	Readers' Circle	Mrs K said to try another book
Missing since Monday	Sep+ 27	Me	pg 41 looks interesting
"	Sept 30	Me	pg 56 getting better
"	Oct 1	Me	finished OK
The Knight and the Dragon	Oct 1	Me and Nick	I got a Buddy Reader Nick. We liked the book
Dying to Know	Oct 2	Me	pg 21 OK
"	Oct 3	Readers' Circle	Too hard to Understand Try another book How about I am Rosemarie
I Am Rosemarie	Oct 3	Me	Very good So far pg 21
"	Oct 4	Me	pg 43 good, getting better
"	Oct 7	Me	pg 63 I love this book
Eyes of The Dragon	Oct 8	Me and Nick	Nick & I read The Eyes of the Dragon We liked the pictures

- Most importantly, hold mini-workshops with the students to help them in their role as effective buddy readers. Issues with which you will need to deal include:
  - how to choose a good book for your buddy;
  - what reading with expression means; how to make the presentation interesting;
  - strategies to use if the younger child becomes restless or uncooperative;
  - how to keep records and fill in the comments in the log book so that more is said than "nice" or "good". The booktalk with which they are becoming comfortable in their Reading Circle will help the students conduct interesting conversations with their younger buddies.

The success of a buddy reading program depends on the collaboration of the two teachers involved and the teacher-librarian. Regular meetings need to be held to discuss the progress of the students and the operational details of the program, and to plan any modifications necessitated by the changing needs of the students.

Home Reading

It is our expectation that our students will take books home from the classroom and the school library. One of our primary objectives is to convince them that reading books is a good way for them to spend their time, at least as entertaining as watching television or playing a video game. We try to help our students develop the habit of reading so that they will become lifelong readers. We want them to see that reading is not just a classroom activity but one that can be carried out anywhere, anytime. To give status to reading at home the following strategy can be used:

- Construct a reading contract as part of your homework expectations. Develop this contract with the students, deciding together what is an appropriate length of time to spend on this activity. Leave the choice of reading materials up to the students. When the class is working on a particular theme or genre, suggest the students might like to borrow from the books you have collected for the theme.

Borrow-a-Book Club

AGREEMENT

I will . . .   enjoy and care for my book;
read for 20 minutes each day;
discuss my book with members of my family;
fill in the comment card.

_____   _____
Student's signature   Parent's signature

In order to gain vital parental support the following strategies have proven successful.

- At a parents' meeting or interview inform the parents of your policy on home reading. If this is not possible send home a letter. In order to involve all the parents, have any communications translated into their languages if they do not speak English. Ask the parents to commit themselves to monitoring the reading done at home. Work on the assumption that parents *are* interested in their children's progress and are willing to be involved. It has been our experience that parents often simply want to be told how to best help.

September 23/91

Dear _____,

It is one of my goals this year to encourage my students not only to perfect their skills as readers but also to enjoy and think about the stories they are reading. In order to do this they need to be immersed in a world of literature at home as well as at school. Thus home reading will be a requirement of our homework policy. Research shows that when parents take an interest in this reading their children do better at reading tasks at school. Thus I would ask both you and your child to sign the following Borrow-a-Book Club agreement and return to me.

Thank you,

_____
Teacher's signature

- Include a comment booklet that parent and student can fill in together. The booklet should have space for the title of each book read, the number of pages read each night, and a parent's initial and comment. Comments may include how well the student concentrates, how much time is spent reading, and any remarks the student may have made about the book.
- Parents who like reading themselves may read aloud parts of books to their children. Although people are comfortable reading to young children they often stop once the children can read for themselves. We believe that adults should go on reading to children as long as doing so brings pleasure to both. We encourage parents to read aloud to their young teenagers. We remind them that we read aloud to the class, and ask them to continue this activity at home, as the sharing of stories often opens channels of communication that might otherwise remain closed. The sharing of stories means the sharing of ideas and values. Some parents may also respond to the teacher by giving *their* opinions of the books their children bring home, and a genuine dialogue can take place.
- Respond to the comments that parents and students make in their comment booklets. If these comments are ignored, then the writing will seem to have little purpose. Your responses can lead to communication from school to home and back again that is of value far beyond the language program. Students see teachers and parents communicating and working together on something that both feel is important; reading is seen to be valued at home as well as at school.
- Be sure to monitor the books that are being borrowed for reading at home. Make suggestions and modifications based on your knowledge of each student. Set aside a time each week to read the booklets, respond to or make any comments, and make necessary adjustments to the program.
- Provide a regular opportunity for parents to learn more about the program, either through evening meetings or through newsletters. Keep on telling them why you do the things you do and how important their role is.

Materials Read During Week of:	Alan has read for 15 minutes most nights this week.
Monday Oct 7/91	*A. Greig* signature.
Diamond Champs	
Sports Illustrated	**Additional Comments:**
Mad Harry	Alan enjoyed these books. They seem a bit easy for him. Are they?
	Not really. This is recreational reading. Mad Harry is a change from sports which he loves. At home reading should be pleasurable. Thanks for your interest *Linda*

Materials Read During Week of:	Alan has read for 15 minutes most nights this week.
Monday Oct 14/91	*A. Greig* signature.
Mad Harry	
Bunnicula	**Additional Comments:**
Stone Fox	We both loved Stone Fox. What a great story this is. Alan wouldn't put it down until he finished it! Got any more??
	I don't think so but I'll get Alan to visit the library. I think he might like Gary Paulsen's books although they are harder to read. Let me know how he gets on with them *Linda*

Home reading programs take classroom time to organize and monitor. They can be seen as an "add-on" that takes time away from actually teaching. We believe that the time spent reinforcing the message that we value reading at home is time really well spent. We try to keep home reading high on our list of priorities and not let it get squeezed out of the timetable. When we place a value on the interactions between parents and students, valuable teaching and learning take place for ourselves as well as our students.

School Bookstores

A school that really cares about literacy is full of book-related activities. Bulletin boards celebrate books and authors; authors visit regularly; the whole atmosphere of the school signals that this is a place where people care about books and reading. One way to increase reading awareness in your community is to organize a school bookstore.

Book ownership is a very different thing from borrowing because it allows the reader to return to a book over and over again. We like to promote book ownership by taking the class on a visit to a local bookstore and by having books from that store available in the school for the students to buy. Having a bookstore right in the school will often put books into the hands of children who might not normally think of owning a book. Parents value the advice that teachers can give regarding the suitability of books for their children, and a school bookstore becomes a focal point in a school for the generation of enthusiasm for books.

A school bookstore is relatively simple to organize:

- First approach a local bookseller and put forward a proposal that you become their agent. You will sell books in your school, at full price, which you will obtain and order through this retailer. You can usually negotiate a small discount; you can use the savings to increase the volume of your stock over time. You will need a small amount of capital to invest in your stock, unless the bookseller will give you the books on consignment. Parent-teacher groups may be willing to lend this start-up money.
- Start with a small collection of sure-fire sellers. Buy books for all the students in the school. The kindergarten parents will be among your best customers as they will be looking for good books to read aloud to their children. Fellow teachers will also spend money to build up their classroom libraries.
- Decide how often to open the store; once a week at recess or during the lunch hour is usually enough.
- Find a location in an entrance hall or foyer that is visible and

used by many people. The books can be kept in a box or cupboard and simply displayed on a table when you open the store.

- Establish a roster of parents and students who will take turns opening the store. Student helpers must be committed to their work and be given status as bookstore personnel through some form of recognition such as badges to wear, the awarding of certificates, and perhaps an annual pizza lunch!
- Make posters and fliers to announce a Grand Opening with balloons and a story reading session. Use the creativity of your students to think of ways to publicize the venture throughout the school and to keep the enthusiasm maintained over time. A regular newsletter announcing new arrivals at the bookstore, and perhaps containing book reviews written by your students during reading workshop time, will help keep the initiative going. It also offers a genuine audience for student writing.
- Open the bookstore on parent evenings and have special events just before Christmas and other holidays.

Running a school bookstore can be enormous fun, but it is also hard work in terms of the commitment you must make. The most successful ventures involve responsible older students who keep accounts and stock lists and take charge of publicity under the supervision of a parent volunteer and a teacher.

The Writing Workshop

Although this is a book about reading, we feel that it is vital for students to write in response to literature. We also acknowledge that it is necessary to provide time for students to write on topics of their own choice as well as in response to books. Such writing includes stories, poems, songs, journal entries, letters, informational writing, and personal reflections.

Nancie Atwell's model of the writing workshop provides a framework for organizing the writing classroom. Everyone writes together. We believe that in order to establish concentration and commitment there should be periods of uninterrupted silent writing. The problem is how to fit everything into the crowded timetable.

Some teachers spend part of each day engaged both in writing workshop activities — keeping notebooks and journals, drafting, conferencing, revising, editing, and sharing student writing —

and in reading workshop activities. Other teachers plan a block of time (a week or a month) that is devoted to personal writing projects. Reading during this time often includes articles by writers on writing and consideration of the writer's craft. Other teachers incorporate a writers' workshop into the timetable only when the students are all reading from books of their own choice. During integrated themes they suspend both the writers' workshop and the readers' workshop in favor of a more integrated approach to reading and writing activities.

The drawback to treating personal writing as a special topic only for a week or a month is that it doesn't provide daily practice at writing on self-chosen topics throughout the year. The disadvantage of a daily writing workshop is that there simply isn't enough time to do everything! Whichever timetable framework you choose for your class, remember there must be daily writing activity, whether it be on student-selected or teacher-directed topics.

During the writing workshop, daily or semestered, entirely student-selected or not, the teacher has various roles. Some time is spent with small groups of four or five talking about how their writing is going. Some time is spent engaged in direct instructions either to the whole class or to small groups drawn together by need. Most of the time the teacher moves around the room, offering suggestions, asking for clarification, and encouraging individuals in their efforts.

Each student has a writing folder in which they store their ongoing work. These folders are kept in a hanging file folder. As they finish each draft, the students meet with their writing partners to read their pieces and discuss the writing. These conferences need to be guided at first, as the students are not automatically effective conference partners. They need help in listening and in knowing how to respond to each other's writing.

A colleague of ours, Val Taylor, suggests the following format for effective peer conferencing. It is first taught to the whole group, and modelled by the teacher in front of everyone. Then, in pairs, students who are confident can model the writing conference while others watch. Eventually, everyone will feel confident about discussing their writing with a friend.

Instructions to give the writing partners:

- Face each other at a table or on the floor and look at the writer as she/he reads.
- Begin by saying what you heard in the writing.
- Ask for clarification of anything that you didn't understand.
- Make a connection between what you heard in the story and something else you know about. "That reminds me of. . ." Connections can be made between this writing and other pieces by the same student; between the writing and the listener's own personal experience; between the writing and books or stories that the class has shared.
- Finish the conference by making one helpful suggestion that the writer can use to improve her/his work and by offering a compliment on something you liked a lot.

This conference echoes the model of response to literature suggested for the Reading Circle. The same attention to detail, to personal connections, and to making meaning is present. We treat our students' writing in the same way that we treat published books in the reading program. We make a personal response.

After the peer conference the students meet with the teacher for a content conference in which they may be asked to revise by adding more to their work or by giving clarification. We have found that many students believe that more means better, and we spend time in mini-lessons and conferences showing them that quality is not necessarily equated with quantity. We try to nudge them gently to new insights about writing through our responses to their work. We expect them to have carried out a first edit for mechanical errors in spelling and grammar before they bring work to us.

When student and teacher are satisfied that the work is finished, it is transferred to a work portfolio. These portfolios are stored in a large file cabinet to which the students have access. A record of finished work is written on the front of this writing folder.

Writing Ideas:

Topic	Date Started	Date Finished	Published
BaseBall Heros	SePt 12	sePt 24	MaYbe
Trivial Pursuit cards on BaseBall	SePt 25	SePt 27	yes
MY famiLY	oct 1	oct 7	
SpookYstory	oct 8	oct 11	Yes
MY DOg	Oct 16	OCT 25	
Hallowe'en story	tues 29	Nov 5	

Once a month the students each select one piece of work that they wish to publish from their work portfolios. This piece must then be edited very carefully, with the teacher being the final editor.

Our writing program has been much informed by the work of Nancie Atwell, Lucy McCormick Calkins, Jane Hansen, and Donald Graves. All these teachers have contributed to our understanding of writing as a craft which must be taught and learned through practice. The organization and day-to-day running of a writing classroom, however, is decided by individual teachers and students to best meet their needs. There is no one right way to do it, no orthodoxies to which one must adhere. We are convinced that the reading program and the writing program are actually one and the same and not two separate entities. In our work we try to help students learn about writing by reading, and learn about reading by writing about books they have read.

Conclusion

These, then, are the building bricks of the program — reading aloud, personal reading, response activities, Reading Circle, using the library, buddy reading, home reading, and writing workshops. But how is everything to be fitted in? It seems an impossible agenda. The students are constantly being withdrawn from class for other programs — French, physical education, music, heritage language programs, and resource support. The curriculum is overcrowded and the timetable is full. In the next chapter we turn to the realities of organizing the timetable. We look at a long-range plan for a year's course of study, at the organization of theme units of differing lengths, and at the activities that can be part of a daily language period.

3   Themes and the Timetable

Subject Integration

Many of the frustrations of teaching are caused by timetables that do not allow for sustained concentration over long periods of time. No sooner is everyone settled and organized with materials, and the atmosphere for work established, than the bell rings and everyone changes focus to another subject. This organization of time is one of the orthodoxies of teaching that we think needs to be challenged. Is this how *we* do our best work, in tiny chunks of time? We suggest that the timetable consider language arts not as a separate subject from social studies, history, geography, and science, but rather as a means to an end. Language learning is common to *all* subjects.

In subjects such as mathematics and science, for instance, students must read, write, and work in small discussion groups to collaborate on projects and solve problems. In all subjects they need to develop the skills of listening, talking, and thinking that are part of language. Language is a medium for learning as much as it is a subject. The more students read and write, the more they will come to know about reading and writing.

We work in broad-based themes derived from literary, social studies, and environmental topics. Some of these themes last from six to eight weeks while others are mini-themes, lasting only two or three weeks. They take different forms, but all operate on the premise that language skills are best learned in meaningful contexts, not in isolation. The objectives the English subject specialists have for the students in terms of their communication skills and appreciation of literature are still being fulfilled, but now these skills are acquired in conjunction with other learning in the content areas. All the students will read and respond to at least one novel, poem, short story, article, or picture book during the study of a theme. They will produce a response to be shared with the group that will enhance the group's understanding of the theme.

When we broaden our definition of language arts to include language across the curriculum, language for thinking, for problem-solving, for communicating and generating new meanings, then we can encompass the objectives of different subject areas within one timetable framework.

Subject integration allows us to buy the time we need for the students to become engrossed and to sustain their concentration long enough to see work come to fruition. It also allows us to vary the mode of instruction, creating a balance between teacher-directed whole class instruction, small-group learning, and independent activities. And it allows us to incorporate drama, music, art, and media studies in an integrated, meaningful curriculum.

We timetable most or all of the morning with the home-room teacher as a block of time for language-related activities in integrated theme studies. Some days this block of time is longer than others, depending on the need to include in the timetable teacher preparation time, physical education, French, and other programs which withdraw students from the classroom. But whenever the teacher has the class together this time is treated as a continuous integrated language time. We read aloud to the students, meet with groups of students in the Reading Circle, model new response strategies, and encourage the students to write on topics of their own choice as well as in connection with the theme. All the time the students spend in their home-room in the afternoon is designated as a math/science time. Activities are planned to allow the students to develop concepts as outlined in our math/science guidelines. We know that as they work at these subjects they develop and use language and communication skills. They read and write, speak and listen regardless of the content under consideration.

Planning the Year by Themes

Having decided how to integrate subjects within the timetable, you will be faced with the responsibility of ensuring that you cover the curriculum. How will you get through all the subject-specific content? How will you deal with the practicalities of integrating work in social studies and other subjects and language arts?

The approach that we have taken is to use a number of broad-based themes throughout the school year. These themes are organized in three distinct formats, in terms of time, materials, and groupings of students. One format — and we always begin with this one — is an independent reading study. A second format involves work in one particular type of literature — mystery, for example, or science fiction — or literature selected because its content relates to a particular theme, such as change or relationships. The third format is the study of a core book, or group of books, which all the students explore through extensive responses.

In the *independent reading study* each student has a book of their own choice to read. Each day a group of six to eight students of heterogeneous ability meet with the teacher in the Reading Circle to discuss their particular book, to offer recommendations to their friends, and to learn the mechanics of booktalk. Meanwhile, the other students are busy with their own response activities.

In the *focused reading study* each student has their own book. All the books have either the same literary or content focus. Some literary themes are mystery, fantasy, humor, myth and legend, adventure, science fiction, and time travel. Social studies themes include changes in children's lives, family relationships, friendship, exploration, the lives of children in other countries, changes in society, conflict, and peace studies. Some environmental studies themes are local environments, global environments, and endangered animals.

In the *core reading study* we work with a smaller number of titles on a narrower, more specific topic. All the students who are reading the same text meet with the teacher once a week in the Reading Circle to discuss the specifics of the plot, the characters, and the author's literary style. Some successful core topics are the War of 1812, cultural heritage and ancestry, and Canada's native people.

There are a number of ways to organize the class for these core reading studies:

- Select fifteen books on the topic and obtain two of each. Have the students work in pairs to create a joint response to each text.
- Select six to eight novels of varying reading difficulty and obtain five or six copies of each. Ask the students to choose which

novel they wish to read. This naturally creates reading groups which meet in the Reading Circle to discuss a book that all the members of the group have read. During the theme study all the students will read as many of the core books as they can.

- Find one novel and read it to the class. You may wish to provide copies for the students so they can follow the reading. Following the text while the teacher reads aloud is an excellent strategy for increasing word recognition and pronunciation. Chapters can be assigned for homework and for reading silently during class.

The *content* of all the themes selected for study is determined by current events, the students' interests, and curriculum objectives. For example, many teachers responded to the Gulf War by introducing peace studies at that time. Mystery is often included in yearly plans as many students really enjoy mystery novels. In order to meet the curriculum objectives of local jurisdictions it is important when planning the year to provide a balance in theme studies between those that explore literary themes, those that are derived from the social studies or history curriculum, and those that complement the curriculum in environmental studies.

The particular *focus* of each of the themes depends very much on the interests and learning styles of the students. We have found that the broader the theme the more successful it is because it affords all the students an opportunity to pursue a line of thinking that is of interest and relevance to them. For example, in one grade six class, the theme was the environment: some students researched the effects of acid rain, others looked at the garbage problem, and others examined the issue of native rights and restrictions on trapping. They all read a wide variety of articles and books in order to research their particular focus.

The *format* the theme takes (independent reading study, focused reading study, or core reading study) depends on the availability of materials and time. If the topic is narrow — for example, the War of 1812 — it is difficult to find enough reading material at the right age and interest level for each of the students to have a different book. Thus a core reading format must be used. Core reading themes usually take less time and fit nicely between the longer, more broadly based themes. Thus we use them to end or begin most terms of work and to fill in short periods of time.

The *order* in which we introduce the themes depends largely on the students' experiences, learning backgrounds, and the time of year. As we have said, it is not possible to spend the whole school year working on major theme units. We plan one big unit each term and a number of less extensive, shorter units to be studied before and after the big one and to reflect specific student interests.

The learning strategies and the response activities are the same in all the theme units. As the year unfolds these are introduced, practised, and developed. We introduce the students to the Reading Circle, to response journals, and to other response activities which will encourage them to explore ideas and demonstrate comprehension. The notion of reading extensively and writing in response to reading, which lies at the core of the work that students will do in each theme, is introduced in September. Individual response activities are taught gradually, beginning with the whole class learning to do something. Eventually the students have a range of responses available to them and can exercise choice and discrimination in deciding which activity best suits the books they have read. The goal is to give the students choice and independence in the work they do in response to reading.

To Begin the Year

We like to begin the school year with an independent reading study unit as it is one way to ensure that the students have the beginnings of a repertoire of successful response strategies available to them for future theme work. We block approximately four weeks for this unit of study. The students are free to select any text(s) they wish from the collection of picture books, magazines, short novels, poetry, and non-fiction materials that we provide.

We use this time to make an initial diagnosis of the students' interests and reading ability. During the unit some students read two or three books, more if picture books and poetry are included, while others read only one. Some books are much longer than others, so the number of books read doesn't tell us much about the students' reading speed and stamina unless we look at the titles and take the difficulty of the books into account. Thus the first activity that we teach the students is how to use a reading log. We insist that the students write in this log each day, and we check the entries and respond to them.

Here is an example of eleven-year-old Kurt's reading log in September.

Title of book, poem read	Date Read	Reader	Comment
The Hit-Away Kid	Monday Sept. 9.	Kurt	I like Matt Christoper pg 12
"	Tues. Sept. 10	"	I'd never bend the rules. Its not fair pg26
The Hit-Away Kid	Wed. Sept. 11	Kurt and Mr. S. (Readers Circle)	Kurt knows a lot about baseball. pg 40 He retold the story well
The Hit-Away Kid	Thurs. Sept 12	Kurt	I finished it!
Harry in trouble	Fri. Sept 13	Kurt	Easy book. I lost my library card too
Nate the Great	Mon. Sept. 16.	Kurt	Easy book
Blackberries in the dark	Tues. Sept. 17	Kurt	Sad. I hava grandpa in Germany
"	Wed. Sept. 18	Reader's Circle Kurt and Mr. S.	talked about memories - assigned a written response
My Cat	Thurs. Sat 19	Kurt and Karl	I got a buddy from Jk. We liked the book.
Blackberries in the dark	Thurs. Sept 19	Kurt	finished! It was o.k. I like sports books beter
The Diamond Champs	Fri. Sept. 20	Kurt	Good so far page 12
"	Tues. Sept 24	Kurt	o.k pg 26
"	Wed. Sept. 25.	Reader's Circle Time Kurt and Mr. S	Understand a story Suggest he read True Story of the first Black Baseball Player
Rosie's Walk	Thurs. Sept. 26	Kurt and Karl	good book

Every day the teacher reads a story aloud and uses this reading as a starting point to teach specific responses. After the reading log, the first response we like to teach is that of a response journal. Here the students are asked to write to their teacher recapping the important parts of the story and offering some insights into what it meant to them. What links did the story have to their own lived experiences? Time is spent discussing the form the journal entry takes, and what makes a successful and interesting entry.

Here is a response from a student in Susan Tiramaco's grade seven class. Notice the form — the salutation, the date, the underlining of the title read, and the signature.

Oct 10 · 1998

Dear Susan,

    I have just finished reading a book by Lloyd Alexander entitled "The Book of Three". The plot was wonderful and exiting, an unclear climax I suppose, but it made me feel like I was the main character.

    The style of writing of Lloyd Alexander was the old style, even though he is a modern writer, a spice to the story, that made me feel like I was there in the times of kings, queens, knights, evil rulers and assistant pig keepers (don't ask, it's a long story). The words are modern, but the style is old.

    I must highly reccomend it to you, or any reader for that matter, for it is a book that can be enjoyed by anyone. It is action packed, humorous, suspensful and the characters feel real, because as well as kings and queens, there are also normal people who have emotions like you or I.

    Anyway, get a copy of the book, take a day to read it. It's definately worth it! I give it a high five, two thumbs up, a ten! It's wonderful! I am now reading the sequel, or part two of the five part series.

            Keep reading,
            Laurent.

Dear Laurent,

I'm convinced ... where's the book!!

                Susan

Three more response activities that we teach during this independent reading unit are: designing a new book cover; making an advertisement or poster; and writing a review.

In designing a new book cover the students are instructed to design a new front cover complete with new illustration and book title. On the back cover the students must write a brief "hook" to whet the reader's appetite. On the fly leaf they must write a short introduction to the author and, where applicable, the illustrator. The example taken is from a student in Mary Klos's grade eight class.

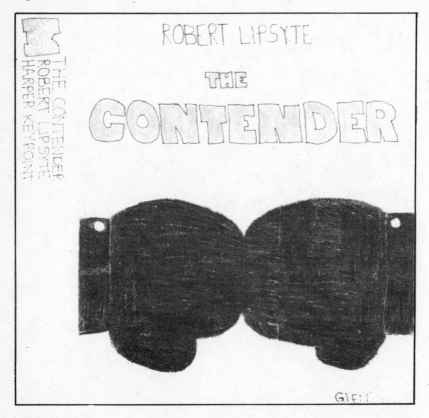

In making an advertisement or poster the students are limited to fifty words. Time is spent examining posters and discussing the importance of visual effect. Bookstores and publishers may be able to supply you with promotional posters that will demonstrate to the students the sort of effect you are striving for. The poster from a student in Linda Melly's grade five class advertises the dog-sled race that is the main event in John Gardiner's novel, *Stone Fox*.

THE NATIONAL
DOG SLED
RACE

place - Jackson, Wyoming

Don't miss it!

This is the Anual dog sled race. It will start and end on Main Street. Any number of dogs may enter. Stone Fox will be there to challenge in the race with his five white samoyed. This year the prize will be $500!! Entry fee is $50.00

In the review-writing activity students first read book reviews in journals and newspapers, such as *Publishers Weekly* and *Quill and Quire*, and in books that review and recommend titles, such as *Michele Landsberg's Guide to Children's Books* and *Choosing Children's Books* by David Booth, Larry Swartz, and Meguido Zola. (Students make another use of these guides in the classroom — they love to see if a book that they have enjoyed "made it" onto a recommended list.)

The review of Chris van Allsburg's *Just a Dream* is from a student in Gary Pruss's grade seven class.

Just a Dream
Chris Van Allsburg
0-395-53308-2

This book is about Walter, a young boy. Walter is a litterbug who considers sorting the garbage into cans, bottles and other to be too much trouble. His idea of the future is based on the Jetsons.

But one night he goes to sleep and wakes up in bed, in several different situations in the future, all of which are horribly polluted. My favorite is on the rim of a huge smokestack belching thick clouds of black smoke. His eyes itch terribly, his throat is sore and he can't stop coughing. Walter asks a workman what the factory makes. The worker explains that the smoke is from the production on Maximum strength Medicine for itchy eyes, sore throats and coughing.

This type of irony is shown throughout the book. The illustrations are truly wonderful. They bring this colourful story to life. All in all I think that Chris Van Allsburg's first environmental book is a great success.

We like these three activities because they involve a synthesis of what has been read, demand writing that is clear, informative, and accurate, and offer the opportunity for artistic expression. The whole class learns these responses together. We use a blackboard or a chart to demonstrate activities related to the story that has been read aloud.

Once the group has learned how to make a particular response, they then apply it to a book they have chosen. Everyone does the same response activity but applies it to the book of their choosing. There is little choice in responses at this stage as we want the students to build up a familiar repertoire. The students do, however, have complete choice over their reading material.

In addition to these response activities we introduce the students to the Reading Circle. We give them the opportunity to learn how to talk about their books. The students meet, once a week, in heterogeneous groups of six to eight students to talk about their books.

By the time this independent reading unit is finished we find the class has settled in, we have some idea of their interests, and we know their reading abilities. We take the next six to eight weeks for the first of our broad-based theme studies, where the literature selected for the students is connected to a theme. We like this format next, rather than a core reading study, because at this time of year we want to continue to give the students choice over their reading materials.

We do, however, limit their choice to books within the theme. The range of materials is as broad as possible, including poetry, short stories, and even plays if we can find them, as well as novels. Some themes that work well at this time of year are mystery, fantasy, folktales, legends, time travel, and science fiction.

After this theme unit is finished we like to end the term with another independent reading study so we can introduce some new response activities, or we use a core novel to explore a specific topic such as celebrations.

We begin the winter term with a very short independent reading study to reorient everyone to the routines of the reading time. We then move quickly into another major theme unit. At this time of year we like to select a theme from our social studies or environmental studies curriculums. Themes that work well at this time of year are friendship, changes in children's lives, heritage and ancestry, family relationships, and understanding conflict. This unit brings us to the end of the winter term.

Following the March break we begin work on a mini-theme, using the format of a core reading study. Some successful themes drawn from the history curriculum are: early pioneers, the War of 1812, and Confederation. Others are native people and the lives of children in other countries. If we want a specifically literary focus we choose a poetry unit or the work of a particular author or group of authors. Contemporary Canadian children's authors whose work offers a rich source of reading are Jean Little, Kit Pearson, and Monica Hughes, among many others. *Canadian Books for Children* by John Stott and Raymond Jones is a good resource for compiling this unit.

At the beginning of April we plan another major theme with everyone reading material connected to a broad-based theme. The content of this unit depends very much on what has gone on in the previous units. We find we usually need to examine the year's curriculum objectives to see what we still need to cover. Some successful topics at this time of year are local environments, global environments, and endangered species.

We end the year as we begin with an independent reading study. This is a chance for the students to select not only their own reading materials, uninhibited by a set theme, but also their own way to respond to their reading. By ending in this manner we are able to observe the changes that have occurred in the students' reading patterns over the past year. This gives us information for the writing of report cards and final evaluation.

We believe the study of themes makes the most efficient use of the students' time because the learning is focused and related. Content is covered, but not at the expense of interest, learning style, and student self-esteem. A successful year plan introduces the strategies gradually, includes a balance between social studies, science, environmental studies, and literary themes, and is sensitive to the developing needs of the students. It encompasses a combination of individualized reading, group novel study, and whole class novel study. As the year progresses it becomes increasingly possible to involve the students in planning the themes and making decisions about their own learning.

A Successful Year's Plan for a Grade Six Class

September	Independent reading study
October to mid-November	Mystery theme (focused reading study)
Mid-November to mid-December	Medieval theme (social studies core reading study)
HOLIDAYS	
January (3 weeks)	Independent reading study
End of January to March	Friendship theme (social studies: focused reading study)
MARCH BREAK	
Mid-March to April	World War II themes (social studies: core novel study)
April to mid-May	Endangered species theme (environmental studies: focused reading study)
Mid-May to June	Independent reading study

Planning a Theme

How to Design a Theme: Time Frames

We have found that most broad-based themes take six to eight weeks to complete, and that within this time period there are four phases. The first phase is the *planning* stage, during which we consult with colleagues, gather materials, and organize the classroom. The second phase, *immersion*, may last up to two weeks. During this time we work hard to orient the students to the theme in question. The students engage in lots of reading and discussion. The third phase, *response*, is the three to four weeks that the students spend carrying out response activities. Finally there is a one- or two-week period during which the responses are shared and individual learning is consolidated through *group* projects. We call this the *wrap-up* time.

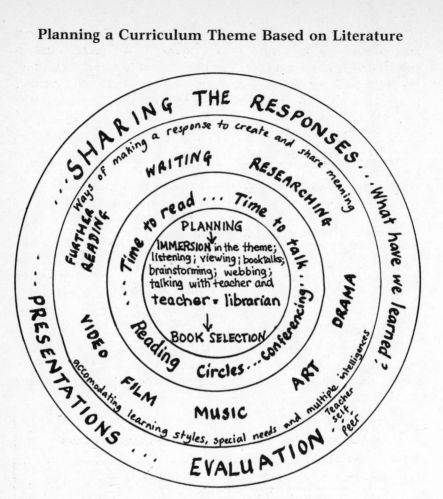

The circle contains, from innermost to outermost:

PLANNING → **IMMERSION** in the theme; listening; viewing; booktalks; brainstorming; webbing; talking with teacher and teacher-librarian → **BOOK SELECTION** — Reading Circles...Conferencing

Time to read... Time to talk...

WRITING — RESEARCHING — DRAMA — ART — MUSIC — FILM — VIDEO — FURTHER READING — PRESENTATIONS — EVALUATION (Teacher, self, peer)

...ways of making a response to create and share meaning — accomodating learning styles, special needs and multiple intelligences

SHARING THE RESPONSES...What have we learned?

**Follow the ideas and activities from
the innermost circle to the outermost.**

A Mystery Unit

Let's take, for example, the literary theme of "Mystery". A colleague decided in late September to explore this topic with his grade five/six class because as he said, "I knew there was a wide variety of juvenile mystery easily available that in the past had been very popular and highly successful with students of this age group. It would also dovetail nicely with the Hallowe'en celebrations that would fall right in the middle of the unit."

He had a number of objectives specific to this theme: he wanted to introduce his students to a large number of books with some common features so that they could discover patterns in writing and recognize formulas; he wanted them to have a greater understanding of how a successful mystery is written; and he wanted them to be able to write their own mystery stories with greater confidence. The work they did during the eight weeks of the theme was related to these objectives. They provided a focus for the collection of information, the discussions in the Reading Circles, and the content of written work, art, drama, and media studies.

Here are some of the steps he took in the planning stage:

Planning

- He arranged a meeting with the teacher-librarian, to plan what activities would take place in the library. It was agreed that during the immersion phase the students would come to the library for a booktalk on available books. During the response phase two activities would take place in the library under her supervision. Each day a different group of students would come to the library for a thirty-minute block of time. Half of the group would try to unlock the secret codes in Graeme Base's book *The Eleventh Hour*. Here is a chart that some teachers find helpful in structuring this response.

Name of Character	Page Character Cleared of Crime
Horace	cooking page
Pig	
Zebra (Eric)	
Rhino	Snakes and ladders page
Swan	
Indian	
Bengal Tiger	Invitation Page
Mouse	
Cat (Cleopatra)	~~Invitation~~ page
The Crocodile (Sam)	Ballroom page
Two Giraffes	Cricket page, Morse code page

The other half of the group worked on the library's computer using the software program entitled *Where in the World Is Carmen Sandiego?*

- With the librarian's help, he found mystery novels and short stories that were at an age-appropriate level and represented a wide range of readability.
- He talked with the other teachers who interacted with the students in the learning centre and English-as-a-second-language classes, and wherever possible they agreed to support the theme by continuing it in their classrooms.
- Together with the students he gathered materials for an attractive display in the classroom. They set this collection up in a corner of the room and labelled it the "Theme Centre". This centre included photographs, newspaper articles about unsolved mysteries, poems, artefacts such as a magnifying glass, and a finger-printing kit. As the theme progressed more material was added.
- The class of twenty-nine students was divided into four heterogeneous reading groups. These formed the Reading Circles. A timetable was posted showing the times each group would go to the library and meet in the Reading Circle.
- He did a needs assessment of the class and decided that the students were now able to use a response journal independently, make a new book cover, design an advertisement for their book, and write in role. He felt from the previous discussions in the Reading Circle that they needed, as a group, more work on assessment of character and retelling of the main ideas of a story. Thus he decided to teach them how to do "Retelling in Six Parts" and a "Wanted" poster.

Immersion

This stage of the work took two weeks. The following activities took place, some in the Reading Circle, others as whole class activities, and yet others as individual activities.

- He met with each Reading Circle and had them brainstorm a list of all the elements/characteristics that are usually present in a mystery story. Here are some examples of their work.

Oct 15,91   The Sluethes

          victim
          motive
          suspect
          crime
          criminal suspect
          stunts
          alibi
          finger prints
          weapon
          action
          crime / problem.

          Private eyes   Wendi
                                    Nancy
      suspence   Claudia
      clues   Robert
      detectives   Alex
      motive   Simon
      weapon
      people
      police
      missing object/person
      violence
      suspects
      crime
      murder
      action

CRIME STOPPERS

MARISA
KELLY
NHON
PAUL

MURDER
DETECTIVE
LIES
SPIES
FINGER PRINTS
EERIE MUSIC
CLUES
PEOPLE.
SUSPECTS
FRAUD
VICTIM

MICHAEL
MARLON

- The groups selected names for themselves and made signs to announce who they were. They called themselves names like the following:

THE SLEUTHS

- He read aloud daily to the class using resources that stimulated discussion. Newspaper articles, picture books, poetry, and magazines were all shared. The students were asked to write responses to these readings in their response journals. The key questions to be answered were, "What did you think about when you heard that read aloud?" and, "What makes a mystery?"
- Because he wanted the students to perfect their retelling skills he also used some of the read-aloud times to practise them. After reading a story he had the group form a circle. He began the story again but stopped after thirty seconds. The person on his right had to continue the story. He clapped his hands at thirty-second intervals to move the story along. When the students felt comfortable with this technique he divided the class into groups of four and had them repeat the exercise. Sometimes the groups had to pretend that they were retelling the story to a stranger who had entered the scene. Other times they had to retell it as if they were one of the characters from the story.
- The film *Rear Window*, directed by Alfred Hitchcock, was shown and the students were asked to record their responses to it.
- The class went to the library for a booktalk to whet their appetites for the books. The students each selected a book to read.
- Time was given for the students to read the books they had chosen. The teacher listened to the students read aloud individually to determine whether or not each book was at the right reading level. There was some negotiation with the students when their initial choices did not seem to hold their attention. The students of course logged their reading daily.
- In the second week of this phase the students were asked to examine the structure of the stories they were reading and to identify each of the characteristics that the group the previous week had identified as necessary elements of a mystery story. They then compared their work and revised their initial list.

Response

This phase of the theme was scheduled to last three weeks. Each week the students had a list of activities that they had to complete. They had the responsibility for completing these tasks independently and in any order they wished. This record sheet helps them keep track of their responsibilities. They are expected to complete all the "musts" and at least one of the choices each week.

WEEK ONE

Musts:

Meet in the Reading Circle.

Make a response journal entry.

With a partner, do a word scramble.

Make a character profile of the detective in your book.

Visit the library and work on the Graeme Base mystery story or the computer program *Where in the World is Carmen Sandiego?*

Choices (at least one)

Design a new book cover.

Design an advertisement.

Write a newspaper account of the crime as if you were a reporter.

Use the fingerprinting kit (see instructions at the end of the unit).

WEEK TWO

Musts:

Meet in the Reading Circle.

Retell a story in six parts.

Visit the library to work on the Graeme Base book or the computer program.

With a partner do a word search.

Choices (at least one):

Design a new book cover.

Make an advertisement.

Write a newspaper account of the crime as if you were a crime reporter.

Make a character profile of the detective in your book.

Use the fingerprinting kit.

Make a response journal entry.

WEEK THREE

Musts

Meet in the Reading Circle.

Make a Wanted poster.

Visit the library to work on the Graeme Base book or the computer program.

With a partner select ten "mystery words" to use in sentences.

Choices (at least one)

Design a new book cover.

Make an advertisement.

Write a newspaper account of the crime as if you were a crime reporter.

Make a character profile of the detective in your book.

Retell a story in six parts.

Make a response journal entry.

Included in the list of "musts" was the time once a week when the students met in the Reading Circle. During these three weeks the focus of discussion was as follows:

WEEK ONE

- The students were asked to brainstorm as a group all the characteristics that they thought a good detective should have. Then they were asked to examine their own book and do a character profile on the detective figure. They were reminded that in a character profile words that describe feelings and actions are put inside the profile and physical characteristics are put outside the profile. These profiles were posted in the room for the other members of the class to see.

WEEK TWO

- The teacher read the group the short story *Nate the Great*. The group decided on the five most important parts of the story. The students were then asked to retell their own stories using the same format. He told the students to divide a piece of paper into six equal parts. The first box was for the title and the last box was for the ending. The remaining boxes were to be used to retell the important parts of the story. The students were instructed to work in the following order: "In the second square put the beginning; now move to the last square and put in the conclusion. Then select three important events from the story and put them in, in order, in the third, fourth, and fifth squares. Illustrate the text and share with a friend."

  The diagram and picture on the next page show this format. Use paper at least 11" by 17" in size.

Story Retelling		
Title And Author's Name 1.	Beginning of story 2.	Three → 4
Other Important Events → 5.	6.	End of Story 3

- The group compiled a list of all the possible rewards that could be used to induce people to offer information about a crime. The students were then asked to examine their own books and design a Wanted poster.

Wrap-Up

Although the teacher had only allotted three weeks for the response stage, as usual the work took longer than expected and actually spilled over into a fourth week. The class then moved on to the last phase of the theme, which includes partner or group work. The students met as one group and brainstormed the following wrap-up activities to pursue:

- Write a mystery story.
- Make a mystery comic strip.
- Research some unexplained mysteries.
- Research the life of a famous mystery writer.
- Make a game using the fingerprint kit. Fingerprint ten people in the class. Write a character profile of each of them. Have the rest of the class try to match each profile with the correct thumbprint.
- Make a new book cover for one of the mystery books. Add a six-part retelling to the inside front cover.

The students selected partners with whom to work and the wrap-up responses they wished to make. Over the next two weeks they worked hard on their responses and practised sharing their responses with their peers. The time in the Reading Circle was spent discussing how the work was going and practising presentations. The students compared their initial assumptions about the characteristics of a mystery with their later views.

At the end of the unit the class shared their work first with their grade one reading buddies, then with an older class, and finally with their parents. Many parents made time to visit the class. They were enthusiastic about the students' commitment to the topic and the skills they displayed in their presentations. The students were now eager to move on to another unit. They had many suggestions to offer!

Other Response Activities

Here are some other responses that can be used in a mystery unit. Many of these ideas are not new, and there are a host of other strategies being tried by teachers and students all the time. Books such as *Literacy through Literature* by Terry Johnson and Daphne Louis, and *Creating Classrooms for Authors* by Jerome Harste and Kathy Short, contain many fine ideas. Other responses are described later as we discuss a fantasy theme, one on changes in children's lives, and one on endangered animals.

The important thing is that the students understand what to do, how to do it, and why they are doing it before they begin. Best of all is when they decide which response they want to make because the book they are reading seems to suggest it to them.

READING CIRCLE ACTIVITIES

- Have the students discuss how one of the main characters in the story they have just read changed. Remember to have them comment on the reasons why the character changed. As a group, have them compile a list of these changes.
- Have each of the students select from their novels the part that they think is the most exciting. Give them time to practise reading this selection. Have them put it on tape for others in the class to use. Have the listeners predict from the selection that has been read how the mystery or crime will be solved.
- Choose twenty significant high content words from a story you plan to read to the class. Reproduce these words and give each pair of students a set of words. Have the students cut the words out and sort them into categories of their own choosing — names, describing words, words that tell about places, and so on. Four or five categories are sufficient. When finished the students talk about their categories and retell their stories around the Reading Circle. They may write their stories if they wish. Finally you read your story.

    This is an excellent strategy for reading words out of context and discussing their possible range of meanings. Credit for this strategy goes to Faye Brownlie et al. in *Reaching for Higher Thought*.
- Read the group a short story, stopping the story at the point when the crime has been described. Now have the group in pairs brainstorm all the possible solutions to this crime. Each pair must record these ideas on a large sheet of paper. When they have finished, have the pairs share their solutions with the rest of the group. End by reading the story to see how the author solves the crime.
- After reading a story have the students choose four places in that story to stop and examine the action more closely. Have the students draw the characters and put thought bubbles above

each character's head. They must write what they think the characters were thinking at these points in the story. Add speech bubbles of what the characters actually said and compare. We call this response *bubble thinking*.

INDIVIDUAL RESPONSE ACTIVITIES

Ask the students to:

- Write about a time in your life when something mysterious happened to you. Describe the experience, what happened, how you felt, and how the experience ended. Share your writing with a friend.
- Make a prediction as to who the villain in the mystery you are reading will be. Record this prediction and your reasons for it in your mystery notebook. Share your work with a friend. When you have read your book check to see if your prediction was accurate.
- In your mystery notebook describe the scene of the crime. Identify what happened and who you think was responsible for this crime. Share your writing with your partner. Have your partner draw your description of the scene of the crime. Then you try to do the same with his/her description.
- In your mystery notebook write how the story would be different if the villain or criminal had been another character. Indicate how the clues that the author put in to help readers unlock the mystery would have to be changed. Share your work with the class or a friend.
- Write a letter to the author, care of the publisher, telling her/him how you felt about the book. Tell how you would have changed the book if you were the author. Share your letter with a friend before you mail it. Remember to include a return address.
- Make a map of the journey that the main characters took in your novel. Use stiff cardboard and markers. Display your work on the bulletin board. Share this work with your classmates.

WHOLE CLASS ACTIVITIES

- Have each student in the class or group make a finger print of the first finger of their left hand using the method described below. Have the students put their fingerprints on small index cards. Now have them add a physical description of themselves (height, weight, eye color, hair color, and sex). Display all these cards on a bulletin board. Number each card. The class must identify all the fingerprints. To check their hypotheses they must make a second fingerprint and compare the two.

Method:
1. On a piece of paper larger than 4 × 5 cm, make a 4 × 5 cm pencil scribble.
2. Press the first finger on your left hand on the scribble.
3. Put a strip of tape, a little larger than the print desired, on your fingertip and press tape on firmly.
4. Peel tape off and place fingerprint on the index card.

• Have each person in the group select five words that they think are important in their story. Each group member must put their words on a list to form a composite list. Then each student must select any ten words to use in one of the following activities.
  • Write each word selected in a new sentence. Remember to check the spelling of the words. Share these sentences with a friend to see if they make sense.
  • Make the ten words that you have selected from the master list into a crossword puzzle. You will need to use a dictionary to make sure the meaning clues you give are accurate. Check your puzzle with the teacher or a partner. A tip: use graph paper and mount on stiff cardboard for other children to use.
  • Use the selected words to make a word search. Check your puzzle with a partner to make sure it is correct. Remember to use graph paper and then put your word search on stiff cardboard for other children to use.
  • Select ten mystery words from the group's list of words. In your novel study notebook write for each word you have chosen as many new words as you can that have the same root word. Share your work with the teacher.

Play the game "Clue". Now design your own cards for this game for others to use.

WRAP-UP ACTIVITIES
• Go to the library with a partner and find all the books that the author of your novel has written. Display these books in the classroom. Make a list of the books. Interview your librarian and find out as much information as you can about the author.

Write to the publisher of this author's work for additional information. Make a poster with all this information to put with the book display of your author's work.

- With a partner select from your novel one feature that you would like to know more about. You might choose a place, a famous character, or a custom. Go to the library and do a mini-research project on this topic. Present your findings to the class.
- With a partner make a diorama of the most exciting part of the story. Write a short explanation to go with it. Use a box, paper of all kinds, modelling material, and found materials to make your diorama interesting to view. Share this work with the class.

Conclusion

Theme studies combine research with the reading of literature. They have oral as well as written components. Most of all allow students to pursue their own lines of inquiry within a broad framework while giving them ideas and challenges with which to become engaged. In the next chapter we offer some additional suggestions for themes which will engage your students in meaningful studies.

4 Additional Themes

Fairy Tales

This theme explores the great stories of many cultures. It has magical qualities!

Immersion Activities

- Brainstorm the characteristics of a fairy tale with the class.
- Read a variety of fairy tales to the class. Discuss the main features of a fairy tale. Remember to include fairy tales from other cultures and more than one version of the same fairy tale.
- Show a video that has a fairy tale quality. Walt Disney has many of the classics on video. Compare these versions with the traditional tales.
- Go to the library with the class and select a range of fairy tales and books that are based on fantasy. Remember to include picture books. Sign out the books for an extended period of time and display in the classroom.
- Have the students select books they wish to read.
- Ask the librarian to discuss with the class how to select a book, how to predict what the book might be about, how difficult the text might be, and how to do a booktalk.
- Before they begin to read, have the students predict who they think the villain will be and the reasons for their prediction.
- Give the students time to read the books before they are asked to respond.
- Have each Reading Circle (a group of six to eight heterogeneous readers) give their group a fairy tale name and make a sign advertising this name.

Reading Circle Activities

- Brainstorm with the group the characteristics of a fairy tale. Some elements to discuss are main characters — villain, hero/heroine, victim; supporting characters; setting — time and place; conflict or problem, and the solution to the conflict or problem. Put this framework on a chart. Have each member of the group use this framework to examine the story they have just read. Compare and contrast the findings.

- Have each group go to the library and find as many different versions of one special fairy tale as they can. Use only picture books. Each member in the group must read one of the books and make a short report to the group. On a large chart compare the story lines of the stories read, the settings of the stories, and the illustrations used by the illustrators. This work could take place in the library under the supervision of the librarian.

- Have the group select either a villain or a hero/heroine, who interests them. Brainstorm all the words that describe this character. As a group, use this word web to write a poem or a chant about the chosen character. Illustrate the poem and share orally with the class.

- Have each member of the group make, on an individual card, a picture of the villain, the hero/heroine, and the victim from the story that they have just read. Then on three separate cards they must accurately write the names of these three characters. Use all the cards produced from the group to form the basis of a concentration game in which the word and picture cards must be matched.

- Read a fairy tale to the group. *Molly Whuppie*, retold by Walter de la Mare, is good for this activity, which is to develop a literary sociogram. To do this have the group identify all the main characters in the story. Place on a chart and draw wide "highways" between characters who have a relationship. Have the students fill in each "highway" with words that describe the feeling/relationship between the two characters. Have them observe if any changes occur in the relationship in the course of the story. Opposite is an example of this kind of group response from a grade four class.

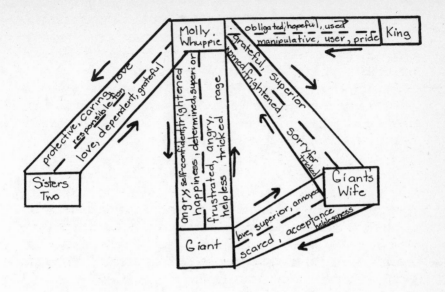

Response Activities

RETELLING

Ask the students to:

- Retell the story you have read using the following technique (see also chapter three). Take a long piece of paper and fold it into six equal parts. In the first square put the name of the book and the author. In the second square write a short recap of the beginning of your story. In the last square write the ending. Now select three important events from your story and put them, in order, in the third, fourth, and fifth squares. Illustrate the text and share your work with your friends.

  Retelling can be done in a variety of ways. Here are but a few:
- Mark off squares on a long, narrow, vertical strip of paper. In each square retell a scene from the story. Illustrate the text. Prepare a television box and thread this "film" through the box. (See illustration on next page.)

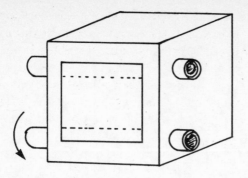

- Draw a map of the journey that the main character/s took. Mark on this map all significant meetings and events.
- Take a long, narrow, horizontal strip of paper and mark off squares. Retell the story using these squares. Illustrate the text. Slide this strip into an envelope with a window cut out and the ends slit open. Remember to work from right to left, not left to right, in this response or it won't work!
- Write a letter to the author of your book care of the publisher. Tell the author how you felt about his/her writing, what the book reminded you of and how you might have changed the book if you were the author. Have your teacher or a friend check your letter to make sure it makes sense.
- Invent a magical animal (like the unicorn, only different. . .). Write a story about it. Sketch a picture of it if time allows.
- Describe your most fantastic dream. What made your dream a fantasy rather than realistic?
- After you have read your book identify the villain in the story. Rewrite the story so that another character is now the villain.
- Write a new ending for the story you have read.
- Make a poster about one of the main characters in the story you have just read. Be sure to place your character in one of the scenes from the story. Include a short biographical sketch of this character. Include in this sketch such information as name, occupation, known friends, and previous history.

Wrap-up Activities

Ask the students to:

- Write a fairy tale for a younger class. Illustrate each page with a picture that will help tell the story more fully. Share your first draft with a friend or the teacher to see if the story makes sense. This is the time to add any information, leave out parts, or change the order. Remember, in a fairy tale there is always a villain, a hero/heroine, a victim, a problem, and a solution. Reread the story to a friend to make sure you are happy with it, then edit for spelling and grammatical errors. Have a friend help you. Now ask your teacher to be your final editor. Publish and share with a younger class.

- Decide on a fairy tale that the group would like to turn into a puppet play. As a group, write an outline of your version of this fairy tale or make up an original tale. The following tasks need to be assigned:
  - turning the outline of the play into a narrative or a script complete with individual speaking parts;
  - making the necessary puppets;
  - making the set.
- Rehearse the play. Be sure that each member of the group has a part. Share the play with the class.
- As a group, read the story *The Paperbag Princess* by Robert Munsch. Now make a game in which four players must work together to save the prince. To begin:
  - brainstorm ten or so obstacles that might prevent a rescue (a river, a dragon, an evil knight, etc.);
  - brainstorm sixteen ways to overcome these obstacles (a boat, a sword, etc.);
  - make a game board with fifty squares showing the path from start to finish;
  - put the obstacles on the game board to block the path;
  - put solutions to obstacles on cards;
  - make the rescuer.

To play:
Deal the cards out to each of the four players. The first player rolls a die and moves the rescuer the indicated number of spaces. When an obstacle is reached the player must put down a solution card. All the players must agree with this solution. If the player does not have a suitable card another player can offer a solution. If no solution is found that is agreeable to all the players the game ends and the prince is not saved. If an agreeable solution is found the next player continues the game until the prince is rescued.

- In a group, go to the library and find as many fairy tales as possible. Each member of the group must select one book to read. Then it is the responsibility of each group member to write a short advertisement for the book that he/she has read. Assemble these advertisements with the books and put on display for the other students in the class to read.
- Plan a fairy tale ball. Decide on a guest list, menu, and story entertainment. Make the invitations. Make the food. Practise stories to be shared. Invite special guests to hear the fairy tales the class has written.

Children during World War II

Students in the late elementary school years have a strong sense of social justice and often develop a keen interest in current events. They ask questions that are often almost impossible for adults to answer, questions about the causes of war and the suffering they see on the television news. One of the functions of literature is to take human experience and view it compassionately through the reflective eyes of the writer. Through stories, a reader can enter imaginatively into events and times other than our own and places far away. The actions and emotions of the characters can be felt by the reader, and we can try to reach an understanding of the motivations and feelings experienced by those people.

The historical events through which we are all living today have their roots in the events of the past. One of the ways of bringing meaning to current events is to examine the historical context through the medium of literature. One of our friends and colleagues, Bruce Singleton, decided to undertake a study of World War II, in recognition of the fiftieth anniversary of the invasion of Poland in September 1939 and the outbreak of the war. He was not looking for a glorification of violence in general, nor of war in particular. Rather, he wanted to focus on how people endure when life has become a nightmare, when deprivation, fighting, and dying are part of everyday events. Together with his teacher-librarian colleague, Marge Kelly, he developed a unit around this theme. Using novels, picture books, and non-fiction materials he introduced his grade six class to the experiences of people, especially children, during the war. The following is an account, of the way he organized and delivered the unit.

Finding Resources

Because of the anniversary there was heightened interest in the topic in the media, so relevant materials in the school library could be supplemented with newspaper and magazine articles. Together, Bruce and Marge gathered a variety of resources that could be used.

They needed to find the following:

- both fiction and non-fiction;
- novels which focused on children's lives;
- material in a range of reading levels;
- multiple copies of titles to facilitate group discussion;
- non-print resources such as maps, pictures, films, and videos.

A thorough search of available books found the following novels that would be used with the class. These "core readings" were obtained in multiple copies so that reading groups could be created. The core books were:

Bilson, Geoffrey. *Hockeybat Harris.* Kids Can Press, 1984.

During the blitz in London many children were evacuated to protect them from bombing. Some of these children went as far as Canada. One such boy was David Harris. In this story he hides his fears and homesickness behind a mask of belligerence, especially towards Bob, the Canadian boy with whom he lives in Saskatoon. The often stormy relationship between the boys is the core of this novel. David's father is in the war in North Africa and the boy's loneliness and fear are hard for Bob to grasp. Bob and the reader both come to appreciate the difficulties David is facing.

Coerr, Eleanor. *Sadako and the Thousand Paper Cranes.* Dell Yearling, 1977.

This story is based on the true story of a little Japanese girl named Sadako. When she is two years old her life in the city of Hiroshima is irrevocably changed. Due to radiation from the atomic bomb, she eventually develops leukemia, from which she dies at age twelve in 1955. While in hospital Sadako is visited by a friend who recounts to her an old story about cranes: if a person can fold one thousand cranes the gods will grant her wish and make her healthy again.

Frank, Anne. *The Diary of a Young Girl*. Random House, 1952.

This book outlines in her own words the short, bittersweet life of Anne Frank, who lived in hiding in an attic in Amsterdam from 1942 to 1944. The story is well known, as is its tragic ending. It forces children of our time and place to appreciate their own freedom and the courage of those who endured such terrible deprivations. This book tells a powerful story and a sad one. It should be used with caution.

Kogawa, Joy. *Naomi's Road*. Oxford University Press, 1986.

Naomi Nakane is a Japanese-Canadian girl whose family loses everything when they are interned in a camp in British Columbia in 1940. This novel deals with the prejudice faced by Japanese-Canadians and shows that Canada had victims of war on her own soil.

McSwigan, Marie. *Snow Treasure*. Scholastic, 1958.

Early in World War II, Germany invaded and subjugated Norway. As part of its resistance effort, Norway smuggled $9 million worth of gold bullion out of the country. The agents of this act of defiance were children! They put the ingots on their sleds and rode by unsuspecting Nazi sentries. This novel chronicles the events leading up to the successful smuggling attempt.

Serrailier, Ian. *The Silver Sword*. Puffin, 1960.

In Warsaw in 1940 three children, aged thirteen, eleven, and three respectively, see their father taken to a Nazi prison camp. While he is held there, their mother is sent to a labor camp and the family home destroyed. Joseph, the father, manages to escape only to discover that his family has been shattered. Seeing a neighborhood boy he offers him a "silver sword", a mere paper knife, with the plea that he look for the missing children. Joseph wants them to know that he is on his way to Switzerland and that they should go there too. The rest of the book describes the children's struggles as they journey alone across war-torn Europe. Although the characters are fictitious the book does describe real experiences endured by children during the war.

A collection of other novels and picture books was introduced into the classroom for supplementary reading. The bibliography appears at the end of this book.

Planning the Activities

Bruce and Marge now sat down together to plan how best to implement the theme. They decided on three components:

- the introduction of the theme through the core novels;
- extension of the theme through research, writing, and listening activities;
- the evaluation of the theme through shared activities.

Bruce always reads aloud to his class every day. During this theme unit he chose Carol Matas's book *Lisa* and its sequel *Jesper*, in which children engage in courageous acts of sabotage in Denmark during the Nazi occupation.

The Core Books

After a general outline of the purpose of the theme unit Bruce introduced the six core books. He explained the approximate reading level of each and discussed a bit of the storyline. Each of four reading groups was to be organized, so that when the Reading Circle met there would be two or more children who had read the same book each time. Some of the books proved to be more popular than others, but with a little sharing and give and take everyone received a copy of one of the core titles. The activities after reading were not specific to the individual titles. They were as follows:

1. The students came to the Reading Circle prepared to talk about their books.
2. They recorded in their notebooks descriptions of the setting and main characters and a brief outline of the plot with predictions about possible outcomes. A class chart comparing and contrasting these features of each of the six books was made and put on display.
3. Each student designed a new book cover or a poster to advertise the book they had read.

Supplementary novels were offered as choices for personal silent reading time. No writing activities were required for them beyond the keeping of a reading log.

Research Activities in the Library

During the theme unit, each reading group spent one period a week in the library. Marge and Bruce developed an activity in which the students designed and made a game similar to "Trivial Pursuit". They composed questions for each other to answer in the game, drawn from their reading about the war. Each student had to write a question and their own name on one side of a card. On the other side they gave the answer and the source of their information. The students had to cross-check each other's work. When the game was played it proved to be a lot of fun and a good way to review the general knowledge acquired by the class.

Writing Activities in the Classroom

During language work periods in the classroom there were two writing assignments to be completed each week. The first was to write a letter from the main character in the book to another character in the book. The second was related to another activity which proved to be one of the highlights of the unit. Marge and Bruce discovered that several members of staff and people within the school community had direct experiences of the war and were prepared to talk to the students about it. The students were asked to think about interview questions they would like to ask survivors of the war. They wrote their questions down, invited the guests to the school library one afternoon, and in small groups conducted their interviews. One staff member had been a child in London during the blitz. A student's grandfather had been captured by the Germans in North Africa, and another grandfather had served on a corvette in the battle of the North Atlantic. Their personal memories brought a very different meaning to the whole topic. Home, school, and history were intertwined, and the unit came to have a personal significance for the students.

Listening Station in the Classroom

Each week, every reading group had one session at a listening station. There were audio tapes of wartime reminiscences, and questions based on the tapes which the students answered in their notebooks. (Recorded excerpts from related books could also have been used for the same purpose.)

Schedule

The schedule for each week of the unit is outlined below. There was a four-day weekly timetable for a variety of reasons including public holidays, school events, and library scheduling. It was not always the same four days; it all depended on the school schedule.

	Group 1	Group 2	Group 3	Group 4
Mon.	listening activity	library research	group discussion	writing activity
Tues.	writing activity	listening activity	library research	group discussion
Wed.	group discussion	writing activity	listening activity	library research
Thur.	library research	group discussion	writing activity	listening activity

Sharing

Sharing of assignments was accomplished in several ways. The entire class listened to a letter written by Avi's grandfather describing his service on a WWII corvette on convoy duty in the North Atlantic. The whole class watched the movie *Miracle at Moreaux* and discussed it. Each of the reading groups talked about their observations of the various characters in the core books. Every pupil wrote a response at the end of the unit on what they had learned from the unit. The charts and artwork were displayed in the classroom and in the hallway.

Evaluation

At the end of the unit Bruce wrote:

> The unit had its strengths, but it also had its weaknesses. For grade six children, the diary of Anne Frank was overpowering. Beyond bravery and courage there was despair and horror. This is not a unit for younger children. Indeed, had I not taught these particular students in grade five the year before, I might not have explored this theme with them in the first term.
>   The unit did, however, offer a realistic picture of war and went some way to counteracting some of the stereotypical ideas of death and glory that the students see on the cinema screen

and in videos. It also combined fiction and non-fiction resources very well. It allowed me to introduce history in a more relevant way to my students. Inviting members of the community into school to talk about their experiences was really successful and is something to bear in mind for other units. Along with another favorite unit, "Medieval Times," "Children during World War II" was a very successful theme and I would use it again.

Endangered Animals, Conservation, and the Environment

This theme explores the changing ecology of the globe and the consequences of change on the balance of nature.

Immersion Activities

- Brainstorm the problems of animal endangerment with the class.
- Read a story to the class that features a main animal character that is endangered. Discuss the nature of the problem and possible solution.
- Show a video or a film with the same theme.
- Ask the librarian to introduce this topic with a booktalk on the available materials.
- Go to the library with the class and select a range of animal-related materials. Sign out these materials for an extended period of time and display in the classroom.
- Have the students select books they wish to read. Discuss with them how to select a book, how to predict what the book might be about, and how difficult the test might be.
- Before they begin to read, have the children write about a pet they have or wish they had.
- Give the children time to read the books before they are asked to respond to them.
- Divide the class into Reading Circles. Have each group name themselves and design a poster telling who they are. Post a schedule of Reading Circle times.

Reading Circle Activities

- As a group brainstorm all the ways that we can help to prevent animals from becoming endangered. Have the children write a short article for the school newspaper telling people how to help prevent animals from becoming endangered.

- Decide as a group the definition of the terms *endangered, extinct,* and *rare*. Now, as a group, make a list of all the animals that you think are endangered, extinct, and rare. Have each group member select three animals to check for proof that they are really endangered or extinct or rare.

- Have each group go to the library and find as many information books as they can about an animal in a read-aloud story. Have the students make a collection of these books for the rest of the class to use in the classroom. List the names of the authors and the titles of all the books. Suggest some questions the other students might try to answer before using the books.

- Have each group select an animal that they know from their reading to be endangered. Have two members of the group investigate the causes of this endangerment. Have them record their findings on chart paper. Have another two members investigate what is being done to stop this endangerment. Have them record their findings. The remaining two members of the group draw or make a model of the animal in its natural environment. Then, as a group, brainstorm ways in which people can prevent further endangerment to these animals. Put all this information on a chart to share with the class.

Response Activities

Assign any of the following:

- Write a letter to the Minister of the Environment. In this letter state your concerns about the environment and pose five questions that you would like to ask about the state of the environment and the animals that live within this environment. Offer some suggestions as to how you would safeguard our environment and the animals that live within it. Send your letter to the Minister of the Environment. (Make sure you give the students the full address, whether it is federal, provincial, or state.)

- Write a letter to the author of your book. Tell how you felt about his/her writing, what the book reminded you of, and how you might have changed the book if you were the author. Have your teacher or a friend check your letter to make sure it makes sense.

- Write a letter of recommendation about the book you have just read. Be sure to "sell" your book to your friends without giving the story line away! Share your thoughts with your classmates by putting this report up on the "good read" board.

- With a partner brainstorm a list of reasons why animals become endangered. Make a poster to illustrate these reasons. Share with the class.
- Make a poster about an animal in the story you have just read. Show the animal in its natural environment. Tell if this animal is endangered or not. If it is, explain the causes of the endangerment. Be prepared to share this poster with your classmates.
- Make a model, using modelling material, of an animal from the story that you have just read. Be sure to place your animal in its natural habitat. Discuss with your group conditions that might be or already are dangerous to this animal. List those conditions on a chart to go along with your model. Be prepared to share your work with the class and to answer any questions.

Wrap-up Activities

Ask the students to:

- As a group select an animal that interests you. Brainstorm all the words that you can to describe this animal. Now use this word web to write a poem or a chant about the chosen animal. Illustrate the poem and share orally with the class.
- With a partner write a short story for a younger class with an animal as the main character. Remember to illustrate each page with a picture that will help tell the story more fully. Share your first draft with a friend or the teacher to see if the story makes sense. This is the time to add any information, leave out parts, or change the order. Reread the story to a friend to make sure you are happy with it. Then edit for spelling and grammatical errors. Have a friend help you. Now ask your teacher to be your final editor. Publish and share with a younger class.
- As a group decide on a family of animals that you would like to research. Write down all the information that you already know about this animal family. Select the most important information and have each member of the group check to see that the information is correct. Record this information on a piece of chart paper. Now have each member of the group draw one member of the animal family. Use the information gathered

and the drawings made to produce a large poster of your animal family to share with your classmates. Be prepared to answer any questions that your friends might have about your work. Be sure to answer the questions: "Is this animal endangered?" "Why or why not?" "What is being done to protect this animal from further endangerment?"

- Work with a partner and write down, in point form, all the information that you both know about an animal from a story. Check this information in the library to make sure that it is correct. Use blank filmstrip and very fine permanent markers and make a filmstrip for younger children. This filmstrip should tell them all about the animal you have chosen. Be sure to read the text to a friend or the teacher before you put it on the filmstrip. Share this filmstrip first with your own class.

    Blank filmstrip may be difficult to obtain. A good alternative is the acetate sheets used for overhead projectors, cut into strips and divided into frames. The students show their "film" by pulling the strip across the overhead projector under a sheet of heavy paper from which a frame has been cut. This way they show only one small picture at a time and can read their commentary.

- In your group compose a rap or a song or a piece of instrumental music to describe one of the animals you have studied. Listen to Saint-Saëns' *Carnival of the Animals* for inspiration. You can make percussion instruments out of simple found materials such as uncooked rice in a yogurt container.

- Work with the members of your Reading Circle and choose an animal that is on the verge of extinction. Decide what is the main reason for this animal's fast approaching extinction. Now have two members of the group write a short play that will illustrate this danger. Have two other members of the group make puppets to illustrate the situation. Have the remaining two members of the group design the set. Rehearse the play. Be sure that each member of the group has a part. Share the play with the class.

Conflict and Change in Children's Lives

This theme explores the feelings of children in situations of conflict.

Immersion Activities

- Brainstorm the different kinds of change that have occurred in the lives of the children in the class.
- Read a story to the class that reflects some kind of change or conflict that has affected members of the class. Discuss the nature of the problem and possible solutions. Consider using newspapers in this unit.
- Show a video or film related to this theme.
- Go to the library with the class and select a range of books that reflect changes in the family and society. Sign out the books for an extended period of time and display in the classroom.
- Ask the librarian to do a booktalk on the materials selected to whet the students' appetite for the topic.
- Have each student select a book that they wish to read.
- Before they begin to read, have the children write about a change that has occurred in their lives.
- Give the children time to read the books before they are asked to respond.
- Divide the group into Reading Circles with members of differing reading abilities. Have each group name themselves and make a poster announcing their name.
- Have the students in small groups or partners brainstorm physical actions that demonstrate conflict (for example, an angry face, a clenched fist, etc.). Have each small group portray a selected physical action for the rest of the group to identify.
- Have the students brainstorm a list of typical situations that involve conflict. Some suggested family situations:
  - There is a lot of pressure in your school to experiment with drugs. How do your parents react?
- Your parents don't want you to buy the most popular brand names in clothes. You don't like to go to school in clothes that are not in fashion.
- You want to return a T-shirt to a store that has a "no-return" policy.
  The students must role-play their solutions in small groups. To lessen the fear of embarrassment, have each group share with only one other small group.

Reading Circle Activities

- Cut a variety of pictures from magazines that show people in conflict. Have each group talk about the pictures and decide what the term conflict means and what causes conflict. Have the students in partners make a list of all possible sources of conflict in their lives.

Examine the list of possible causes of conflict and discuss how people react to conflict. Make a list of words that describe these reactions to change and conflict. In partners draw a scene that represents one word that signifies conflict.

- Brainstorm with the group the conflict situations that are present in the novel they are reading. Place these situations in one of the following categories of conflict:
  - Individual against Nature;
  - Individual against Individual;
  - Individual against Oneself;
  - Individual against Technology;
  - Individual against Society.

Have each student keep an ongoing list in their novel study notebook of all instances of conflict and the appropriate category it belongs in.

- Brainstorm in the group how characters in a story might change and why. Have each group member select one of the main characters from their novel and describe in writing what that character was like at the beginning of the story and how she/he changed as the story progressed. Remind the students to explain what caused these changes and to comment not only on changes in appearance but also on changes in feelings and thinking. Share this work at the end of the cycle or day.

Response Activities

CHARACTER-RELATED:

Ask the students to:

- Choose one of the main characters from your novel. Draw a silhouette of this character. List one strength and one weakness of the character. Then select one quote from your novel that would enable you to immediately identify the character, simply from reading the quote. Share this work with your group.
- Imagine an article of clothing that one of the characters in your novel would enjoy wearing. Name this character, draw the

clothing, explain where he/she would get it, estimate its cost, and tell why the character would like it.

- Write down an imaginary interview between yourself and a character in your novel. The interview must contain five questions and answers. Share your work with the group or a friend.
- One of the characters in your book is going to give a speech. You must introduce him/her to the audience. Tell the audience about your character and why they should listen to him/her. Draw a picture to go with this introduction.

Select a character (A) from your novel. Have this character write a letter to someone else mentioned in the story (B). The letter must complain about something or ask for help or tell about a problem in the story. Then Character B must reply to the letter from Character A. You may illustrate these letters. Please remember to check spelling and punctuation and write in letter form.

LITERARY SOCIOGRAM:

- Make a literary sociogram of the relationship between the main characters in the material you are reading. (Remember, always model this technique with the whole class before having them do one on the novel they are reading.)
- Choose a character from your novel whom you would most like to meet. Explain why.
- Compare two characters from the novel you are reading or from two different novels you have recently read. Tell how they are the same and how they are different. Tell which character you most admire and why. Share this work with the group.

PLOT-RELATED:

- Sketch a map that includes the special places mentioned in your novel. Make a "footstep" picture showing the places the main character or characters visited in the correct order. Share this work with the group.
- Draw a picture of a room or building described in your novel that is important to the plot. Write a short caption telling where it is and why it is important to your novel. Share this work with the group or a friend.
- Make a comic strip that tells the most important events in your book. Use speech bubbles for dialogue. The example on the next page is a retelling of highlights from *Call It Courage* by

Armstrong Sperry. It is the work of a student in Linda Mully's grade five classroom.

PROBLEM-SOLVING:

- Fold a paper in four. Read your novel until a problem or conflict occurs. Stop the story. Tell a partner the plot so far. Together, brainstorm four possible solutions to the conflict. Now finish reading the story and share the author's solution to the conflict.
- Identify one of the main conflicts/problems that occurred in your novel. On a time line, record the events that led up to the conflict, what major events occurred during the climax of the conflict, and how the conflict was resolved. Share this work with the group. Remember to identify your novel.
- Locate and clip words from the newspaper to form a headline that tells something about the conflict that occurred in the novel you are reading. Now write a brief story telling your readers what happened during one exciting part of the story. Your editor has limited you to fifty words. Remember to include who, what, where, when, why, how . . . and a picture.
- The order in which events occur is very important to any story.

Choose eight major events in the story and write a short description. Then put on an illustrated time line.

- Weather often plays a part in a novel even if it is just to set the scene. Describe the weather in one important scene and tell why it is important to the story. Illustrate this scene.
- Take a large piece of paper and divide it in half. On the top portion of the paper write about the major incident of conflict from your novel. On the bottom half of the paper show how this conflict was resolved. Offer some alternative solutions for consideration.

SKILLS-RELATED:

- Open your novel to any page and find the name of an object on it. This becomes the title of a list. Under the title list ten common and uncommon uses for your object. Illustrate the most unusual use. Share your work with a friend or your group.
- List at least twelve words that are emotion or feeling words from your novel. Circle five of the most interesting. Try to use these five words in just two sentences.

GENERAL RESPONSES:

- Make a new book cover for the book you have just read.
- Make a poster advertising your book.

Wrap-up Activities

- Create a "Conflict" game. In small groups or pairs brainstorm situations from your own lives that cause conflict. Put these problems on file cards. To play the game, place all the cards in a pile face down in the middle of the table. The first player must pick up a card, read it to the group, and offer a solution to the problem. Then the rest of the group must vote on the solution. A yes vote is a "thumbs up" sign and a no vote is a "thumbs down" sign. To start the vote the player says, "Ready, set, vote." On vote all players show their votes. The no votes are subtracted from the yes votes to get each individual's points. The player with the most points wins.
- Work with a partner and decide on a source of conflict. Depict this conflict in a diorama. Write how this conflict can be resolved.
- Working with a partner or a small group, decide on a major

source of conflict in the world today. Design a poster that illustrates this conflict. Write an editorial outlining how you, as a pair or group, would resolve this conflict.

- Select a source of conflict in the world today. Research how this conflict developed and how it is being addressed. Present your findings to the class in an interesting fashion.
- Make a video that shows how the students of your school can attack a problem that affects them all — e.g., racism, pollution, vandalism.

Conclusion

In this book we have described an integrated language arts program structured around themes. Underlying the practical suggestions are the beliefs that guide our practice: that the curriculum should be relevant to our students' interests as well as needs, and that teaching and learning are multi-dimensional. There is an interconnectedness to everything we do in the classroom. Beginning with our view of our students, which we hope respects their individual learning styles and needs, we try to create a program which involves them at every stage. They help us in the planning of activities and in setting their own goals. They track their reading and response activities, taking responsibility as individuals and as members of the small groups for the completion and self-evaluation of their work.

We believe that student choice and involvement in planning and evaluating learning experiences help us to design a program that meets all their needs. It is not an obstacle course over which all must jump regardless of ability, interests, or inclination. It is a process of negotiation in which students and teachers plan appropriate experiences for everyone. From this process we hope that our students will derive satisfaction as well as knowledge and that they will grow into emotionally secure and socially responsible adults.

This does not mean that our standards are not high. We set our expectations through direct teaching, demonstration, and modelling.

When we read aloud, talk about what we have read, and participate in the Reading Circle, we show students the things we value. When we talk about our reading and writing we set a standard. Learning is a lifelong process and we want our students to know that we are learners too.

There are mechanical language skills that students in grades five through eight are beginning to master. Grammar, punctuation, spelling, and the use of dictionaries and thesauri are part of our program, though in this book we have not explored them in detail. Mini-lessons, word games, and skills practice activities such as crossword puzzles and word searches may all be used to help students master the mechanics of written language. Most effective, however, is the expectation that writing will be done daily, that it will be revised and the content carefully considered before proofreading. Students should proofread and correct their own work as well as helping each other. We learn to write by writing, and the use of dictionaries to develop spelling and vocabulary should be made in the context of meaningful writing assignments.

We hope this book will help you the teacher plan and organize an interactive, resource-based language arts program that offers students a wide range of reading experiences. The bibliographies that follow are intended to offer a starting point as you begin to collect literature for your program. As time goes by you will discover favorites of your own. The exciting thing about teaching with literature is that the program never stands still or becomes stale. It is dynamic and constantly surprising as each generation of students makes their own personal discoveries through books. Add to our lists, design your own theme units, and seek out the literature connections. Enjoy!

Bibliographies

Mystery and Adventure

In this unit the students explore the mystery novel and look for common features from one book to the next. Some of the titles below are from series written by very popular writers and this unit is one that is often very successful in "hooking" reluctant readers into the program. There are a number of very easy-to-read titles in this list, so it makes a good starting point for a younger class or for a first unit in September. For books that are available through additional or different publishers in the United States, we have noted the relevant publishing information in brackets.

Adler, David A. *Cam Jansen and the Mystery of the Monkey House*. Dell, 1985 (other titles available in the series). (Puffin, 1991.)
_____. *The Fourth Floor Twins and the Disappearing Parrot Trick*. Puffin, 1987 (other titles available in the series).

Alexander, Wilma E. *Old Coach Road*. Overlea House, 1987.

Base, Graeme. *The Eleventh Hour*. Stoddart, 1988. (Abrams, 1990.)

Bellairs, John. *The Curse of the Blue Figurine*. Bantam, 1984.
_____. *The Eyes of the Killer Robot*. Bantam, 1987.
_____. *The Figure in the Shadows*. Bantam, 1975. (Dell, 1977.)
_____. *The House with a Clock in Its Walls*. Bantam, 1973. (Dell, 1974.)
_____. *The Spell of the Sorcerer's Skull*. Bantam, 1985.

Brenner, Barbara. *Mystery of the Plumed Serpent*. Bullseye Books, 1981. (Knopf, 1989.)

Cameron, Ann. *Julian, Secret Agent*. Random House, 1988.

Christian, Mary. *Sebastian (Super Sleuth) and the Secret of the Skewered Skier*. Pocket, 1989. (Macmillan, 1984.)

Crook, Marion. *Hidden Gold Mystery*. Overlea House, 1987.
_____. *Payment in Death*. Overlea House, 1987.
_____. *Stone Dead*. Overlea House, 1987.

Doyle, Brian. *Angel Square*. Groundwood, 1984.

Giff, Patricia Reilly. *The Secret at the Polk Street School*. Dell, 1987.

Gordon, Sarah. *The Dangerous Dollhouse*. Stoneberry Books, 1988.
_____. *Eyes of the Lion*. Stoneberry Books, 1988.

Hoban, Lillian. *The Case of the Two Masked Robbers*. Harper & Row, 1988. (HarperCollins, 1988.)

Lawrence, James. *Binky Brothers, Detectives*. Harper & Row, 1978. (HarperCollins, 1978.)

Lively, Penelope. *The Revenge of Samuel Stokes*. Puffin, 1983.

Maccarone, Grace. *The Return of the Third-Grade Ghosthunters*. Scholastic, 1989.

Mackay, Claire. *The Minerva Program*. James Lorimer & Co., 1984.

Markham, Marion. *The Birthday Party Mystery*. Avon, 1990.

Newman, Robert. *The Case of the Baker Street Irregular*. Atheneum, 1984. (Macmillan, 1984.)

Parish, Peggy. *Clues in the Woods*. Dell, 1980.
_____. *The Ghosts of Cougar Island*. Dell, 1986.
_____. *Key to the Treasure*. Dell, 1980.
_____. *Pirate Island Treasure*. Dell, 1981.

Pinkwater, Daniel. *The Muffin Fiend*. Bantam Skylark, 1986. (Lothrup, 1986.)

Quackenbush, Robert. *Sherlock Chick and the Peekaboo Mystery*. Parents' Magazine, 1987. (Putnam, 1990.)

Raskin, Ellen. *The Mysterious Disappearance of Leon (I mean Noel)*. Puffin, 1989.
_____. *The Westing Game*. Avon, 1984.

Saunders, Susan. *The Mystery of the Hard Luck Rodeo*. Random House, 1989.

Sharmat, Marjorie. *Nate the Great*. Dell, 1977.
_____. *Nate the Great and the Sticky Case*. Dell, 1981.
_____. *Nate the Great Goes Undercover*. Dell, 1978.

Van Allsburg, Chris. *The Mysteries of Harris Burdick*. Houghton Mifflin, 1984.

Weir, Joan. *Balloon Race Mystery and Other Stories*. Overlea House, 1988.

_____. *Ski Lodge Mystery and Other Stories*. Overlea House, 1988.

Wilson, Eric. *Disneyland Hostage*. Clarke Irwin, 1982.

_____. *The Kootenay Kidnapper*. Collins, 1983.

_____. *Murder on the Canadian*. Clarke Irwin, 1976.

_____. *Terror in Winnipeg*. Clarke Irwin, 1979.

Folk and Fairy Tales

This bibliography lists illustrated folk and fairy tales. The stories vary in their length and readability level, so there should be something for everyone to read with success. Teachers will also find collections of folktales in the school library as well as versions of many traditional tales in anthologies.

We have sought tales from a diversity of cultures but have deliberately not included the myths and legends of North American native peoples. The focus of the work in our fairy tale unit is on fantasy and the imagination, rather than on the issues which are found in the stories of native North Americans. These should be studied at a different time and in a different context which allows for exploration of the cultures from which they arise.

Ahlberg, Janet and Allan. *Jeremiah in the Dark Woods*. Puffin, 1990.

Aiken, Joan, and Alan Lee. *The Moon's Revenge*. Knopf, 1988.

Alexander, Lloyd. *The King's Fountain*. Unicorn, 1989. (Dutton, 1989.)

Andersen, Hans Christian. *The Snow Queen*. Retold by Amy Ehrlich. Pied Piper, 1982. (Puffin, 1982.)

Day, David, and Mark Entwistle. *The Sleeper*. Doubleday, 1990. (Ideals, 1990.)

de la Mare, Walter. *Molly Whuppie*. Puffin, 1985. (Farrar, Straus, & Giroux, 1983.)

de Paola, Tomie. *Helga's Dowry*. Harcourt Brace Jovanovich, 1977.
_____. *Strega Nona*. Prentice-Hall, 1975. (Simon and Schuster, 1979.)

Downie, Mary Alice. *The Buffalo Boy and the Weaver Girl*. Quarry Press, 1989.

Ehrlich, Amy, and Susan Jeffers. *Thumbelina*. Dial, 1985.

Faulkner, Jack. *Jack and the Beanstalk*. Scholastic, 1986.

French, Fiona. *The Princess and the Musician*. Evans, 1981.
_____. *Snow White in New York*. Oxford University Press, 1990.

Gackenbach, Dick. *The Princess and the Pea*. Puffin, 1986.

Galdone, Paul. *The Gingerbread Boy*. Houghton Mifflin, 1983.

_____. *Jack and the Beanstalk*. Clarion Books, 1974. (Ticknor & Fields, 1982.)

_____. *Three Billy Goats Gruff*. Clarion Books, 1973. (Ticknor & Fields, 1981.)

_____. *Three Little Kittens*. Clarion Books, 1986. (Ticknor & Fields, 1988.)

Gentleman, David, and Russell Hoban. *The Dancing Tigers*. Red Fox, 1990.

Grimm, Jacob and Wilhelm. *Little Red Riding Hood*. Adapted by Trina Schart Hyman. Holiday House, 1982.

_____. *Little Red Riding Hood*. Retold by Tony Ross. Puffin, 1981.

_____. *Rapunzel*. Adapted by Barbara Rogasky. Holiday House, 1982.

_____. *The Sleeping Beauty, from the Brothers Grimm*. Adapted by Trina Schart Hyman. Little, Brown, 1977.

_____. *Snow White*. Adapted by Trina Schart Hyman. Little, Brown, 1974.

_____. *The Twelve Dancing Princesses*. Illustrated by Errol LeCain. Viking, 1978.

_____. *The Twelve Dancing Princesses*. Adapted by Janet Lunn. Methuen, 1980.

Heyer, Marilee. *The Weaving of a Dream*. Viking, 1986.

Huck, Charlotte, and Anita Lobel. *Princess Furball*. Scholastic, 1989. (Greenwillow, 1989.)

Hughes, Monica, and Brenda Clarke. *Little Fingerling*. Kids Can Press, 1989.

Jeffers, Susan. *Wild Robin*. Unicorn, 1986. (Dutton, 1986.)

Louie, Ai-Ling, and Ed Young. *Yeh-Shen: A Cinderella Story from China*. Philomel, 1982. (Putnam, 1990.)

Mayer, Marianna, and Katie Thamer. *The Black Horse*. Pied Piper, 1987. (Dial, 1987.)

Mayer, Mercer. *East of the Sun and West of the Moon*. Four Winds Press, 1980. (Macmillan, 1987.)

McDermott, Gerald. *Anansi the Spider*. Henry Holt, 1981.

Mosel, Arlene. *The Funny Little Woman*. Dutton, 1972.

Muller, Robin. *Little Kay*. Scholastic, 1988.
_____. *The Lucky Old Woman*. Scholastic, 1987.
_____. *Mollie Whuppie and the Giant*. Scholastic, 1982.
_____. *The Sorcerer's Apprentice*. Kids Can Press, 1985.
_____. *Tatterhood*. Scholastic, 1984.

O'Connor, Jane. *The Teeny Tiny Woman*. Random House, 1986.

Sans Souci, Robert. *The Song of Sedna*. Doubleday, 1989.

Scieszka, Jon. *The True Story of the Three Little Pigs*. Viking, 1989.

Sciescka, Jon, and Steve Johnson. *The Frog Prince, Continued*. Viking, 1991.

Steptoe, John. *Mufaro's Beautiful Daughters*. Lothrop, 1987.

Wiesner, David, and Kim Kahn. *The Loathsome Dragon*. G.P. Putnams, 1987.

Williams, Jay, and Mercer Mayer. *Everyone Knows What a Dragon Looks Like*. Four Winds Press, 1976. (Macmillan, 1984.)

Wolkstein, Diane, and Ed Young. *8,000 Stones: A Chinese Folktale*. Doubleday, 1972.
_____. *White Wave: A Chinese Tale*. Crowell, 1979. (HarperCollins, 1979.)

Wolkstein, Diane, and Robert Andrew Parker. *The Magic Wings: A Tale from China*. Dutton, 1986.

Wood, Audrey and Don. *Heckedy Peg*. Harcourt Brace Jovanovich, 1987.

Yagawa, Sumiko. *The Crane Wife*. Translated by Katherine Paterson. William Morrow, 1981.

Yolen, Jane. *Dove Isabeau*. Harcourt Brace Jovanovich, 1989.

Young, Ed. *Lon Po Po: A Red Riding Hood Story from China*. Philomel, 1990. (Putnam, 1989.)

Children during World War II

This unit includes novels that require considerable reading experience and maturity. All the books need to be read in conjunction with regular guided discussion in the Reading Circle. Students may encounter the reality of the Holocaust for the first time through books such as *Freidrich* and *The Devil's Arithmetic*. Teachers should be prepared to engage in discussion which clarifies understandings and which supports young readers in an exploration of their feelings of outrage. An article by Vicki Zack, "It Was the Worst of Times: Learning about the Holocaust through Literature," in *Language Arts*, Volume 68, Number 1, January 1991, is of help to teachers contemplating this unit. She describes the experience that she had with her grade five class as they tried to understand the Holocaust.

NOVELS

Bilson, Geoffrey. *Hockeybat Harris.* Kids Can Press, 1984.

Cooper, Susan. *Dawn of Fear.* Aladdin Books, 1970. (Macmillan, 1989.)

DeJong, Meindert. *The House of Sixty Fathers.* Harper & Row, 1956. (HarperCollins, 1987.)

Greene, Bette. *Summer of My German Soldier.* Bantam, 1984.

Hautzig, Esther. *The Endless Steppe.* Harper & Row, 1968. (HarperCollins, 1987.)

Kerr, Judith. *When Hitler Stole Pink Rabbit.* Lions, 1989. (Dell, 1987.)

Kogawa, Joy. *Naomi's Road.* Oxford University Press, 1988.

Levoy, Myron. *Alan and Naomi.* Harper & Row, 1977. (HarperCollins, 1987.)

Lowry, Lois. *Number the Stars.* Houghton Mifflin, 1989. (Dell, 1990.)

Magorian, Michelle. *Back Home.* Harper & Row, 1984. (HarperCollins, 1984.)

————. *Goodnight Mister Tom.* Viking, 1981. (HarperCollins, 1986.)

Matas, Carol. *Jesper.* Lester & Orpen Dennys, 1987.
_____. *Lisa.* Lester & Orpen Dennys, 1989.

Moskin, Marietta D. *I Am Rosemarie.* Dell, 1987.

Orgel, Doris. *The Devil in Vienna.* Penguin, 1988. (Puffin, 1988.)

Paton Walsh, Jill. *Fireweed.* Puffin, 1972. (Farrar, Straus, & Giroux, 1988.)

Richter, Hans Peter. *Freidrich.* Puffin, 1987.
_____. *I Was There.* Puffin, 1987.

Senje, Sigurd. *Escape!* Harcourt, Brace & World Inc., 1964.

Uchida, Yoshiko. *Journey Home.* Atheneum, 1978. (Macmillan, 1982.)

Yolen, Jane. *The Devil's Arithmetic.* Viking, 1988. (Puffin, 1990.)

PICTURE BOOKS

Eco, Umberto. *The Three Astronauts.* Harcourt Brace Jovanovich, 1989.

Innocenti, Robert. *Rose Blanche.* Creative Education, 1985.

Morimoto, Junko. *My Hiroshima.* Viking, 1987.

Watts, Bernadette. *Varenka.* North South Press, 1981.

Ziefert, Harriet. *A New Coat for Anna.* Knopf, 1986.

BIOGRAPHY AND HISTORY

Abells, Chana Byers. *The Children We Remember.* Greenwillow, 1986.

Bull, Angela. *Anne Frank.* Hamilton, 1984.

Leigh, Vanora. *Anne Frank.* Wayland, 1985.

Marulti, Toshi. *Hiroshima No Pika.* Lothrop, 1980.

Santor, Donald M. *Baachan! Geechan! Arigato: A Story of Japanese Canadians at War, 1939-1945.* Momili Health Care Society, 1989.

Siegel, Aranka. *Upon the Head of a Goat: A Childhood in Hungary, 1939-1945.* Farrar, Straus & Giroux, 1981.

Takashima. *A Child in Prison Camp.* Tundra, 1991.

Endangered Animals, Conservation, and the Environment

In this unit the students explore issues surrounding the threat to the environment from pollution and the over-exploitation of the earth's resources. There is a particular emphasis on endangered animals and the causes of their endangerment. Students are encouraged to feel that through concerted effort and social action we can avert the threatened catastrophes. The books cited are all connected to the theme in some way, either directly or indirectly. Some simply make the point that the world and its creatures are beautiful and that natural beauty is a cause for celebration and wonder. Many of these are picture books, making this a very successful unit for less experienced readers.

Aardema, Verna. *Bringing the Rain to Kapiti Plain.* Dial, 1983.

Alexander, Lloyd. *The King's Fountain.* Unicorn, 1989. (Dutton, 1989.)

Baker, Jeannie. *Home in the Sky.* Greenwillow, 1984.
_____. *Through the Window.* Greenwillow, 1991.
_____. *Where the Forest Meets the Sea.* Greenwillow, 1988.

Banks, Martin. *Conserving Rainforests.* Wayland, 1989. (Steck-Vaughn, 1990.)

Base, Graeme. *Animalia.* Stoddart, 1987. (Abrams, 1991.)

Baylor, Byrd. *Everybody Needs a Rock.* Charles Scribner, 1974. (Macmillan, 1985.)
_____. *I'm in Charge of Celebrations.* Charles Scribner, 1986. (Macmillan, 1986.)

Beasley Murphy, Barbara. *Annie and the Animals.* Bantam, 1989.

Bonners, Susan. *Panda.* Delacorte Press, 1978. (Dell, 1988.)

Burford, Della. *The Magical Earth Secrets.* Western Canada Wilderness Committee, 1990.

Burningham, John. *Hey! Get Off Our Train.* Jonathan Cape, 1989. (Crown, 1990.)

Carrick, Donald. *Harald and the Great Stag.* Clarion Books, 1988. (Houghton Mifflin, 1990.)

Cherry, Lynne. *The Great Kapok Tree: A Tale of the Amazon Rain Forest.* Gulliver Books, 1990. (Harcourt Brace Jovanovich, 1990.)

Cooney, Barbara. *Island Boy.* Viking, 1988. (Puffin, 1991.)
_____. *Miss Rumphius.* Viking, 1982. (Puffin, 1985.)

Cowcher, Helen. *Antarctica.* Andre Deutsch, 1990. (Farrar, Straus, & Giroux, 1990.)
_____. *Rain Forest.* Corgi, 1991. (Farrar, Straus, & Giroux, 1990.)

Davies, Kay, and Wendy Oldfield. *Waste.* Wayland, 1990.

Dorfman, Gillian. *World Wildlife Fund: Our World in Danger.* Ladybird, 1989.

Ehlert, Lois. *Growing Vegetable Soup.* Harcourt Brace Jovanovich, 1990.

Farley, Walter. *The Black Stallion.* Random House, 1969. (Knopf, 1991.)

Gardam, Jane. *Bridget and William.* Puffin, 1984.

Giono, Jean, and Frederic Back. *The Man Who Planted Trees.* CBC Enterprises, 1989. (Chelsea Green, 1987.)

Glimmerveen, Ulco. *A Tale of Antarctica.* Scholastic, 1990.

Godkin, Celia. *Wolf Island.* Fitzhenry and Whiteside, 1989.

Hall, Lynn. *Danza!* Aladdin Books, 1981. (Macmillan, 1989.)

Harranth, Wolf, and Winifred Opgenoorth. *Isn't It a Beautiful Meadow?* Oxford University Press, 1985.

Herriot, James. *Bonny's Big Day.* Piper Books, 1987. (St. Martin, 1991.)

Horton, Penny, Tony Potter, and Dee Turner. *Earth Watch.* BBC Books, 1990.

Hurd, Edith Thacher. *Song of the Swallow.* Little, Brown, 1988.

Ingpen, Robert, and Margaret Dunkle. *Conservation: A Thoughtful Way of Explaining Conservation to Children.* Macmillan, 1988.

James, Barbara. *Waste and Recycling.* (Other titles in the "Conserving Our World", series include *Acid Rain, Conserving Rainforests, Conserving the Atmosphere, Protecting Wildlife, The Spread of Deserts, Farming and the Environment, Protecting Oceans).* Wayland, 1989. (Steck-Vaughn, 1990.)

Jenkins, Alan C. *The Ghost Elephant.* Puffin, 1987.

Kessler, Deirdre. *Lobster in my Pocket.* Ragweed Press, 1988.

Little, Jean. *Lost and Found.* Puffin, 1988.

Lottridge, Celia Barker, and Ian Wallace. *The Name of the Tree.* Groundwood, 1989. (Macmillan, 1990.)

Mattingley, Christobel. *Duck Boy.* Puffin, 1985. (Macmillan, 1986)

Mayne, William. *A House in Town.* Walker Books, 1984. (Simon & Schuster, 1988.)

McCall Smith, Alexander. *Akimbo and the Elephants.* Mammoth, 1990.

Morey, Walt. *Kavik, the Wolf Dog.* Scholastic, 1989.

Mowat, Farley. *Owls in the Family.* McClelland & Stewart, 1990. (Bantam, 1985.)

Muller, Jorg, and Jorg Steiner. *The Sea People.* Victor Gollancz, 1982.

O'Dell, Scott. *Island of the Blue Dolphins.* Dell, 1987. (Houghton Mifflin, 1990.)

Peet, Bill. *Farewell to Shady Glade.* Houghton Mifflin, 1984.

Politi, Leo. *Song of the Swallows.* Aladdin Books, 1987. (Macmillan, 1987.)

Scholes, Katherine. *The Boy and the Whale.* Puffin, 1987.

Smucker, Barbara. *Jacob's Little Giant.* Puffin, 1989.

Steig, William. *Amos and Boris.* Puffin, 1984.

Stone, Lynne. *A New True Book: Endangered Animals.* Children's Press, 1984.

Suzuki, David. *Looking at the Environment.* General, 1990.

Van Allsburg, Chris. *Just a Dream.* Houghton Mifflin, 1990.

Wagner, Jenny. *Goanna.* Viking, 1988.

Waterton, Betty. *A Salmon for Simon.* Meadow Mouse Paperback, 1990. (Camden, 1991.)

Wexo, J.B. *Endangered Animals.* Wildlife Education, 1986. (Creative, 1989.)

Wheatley, Nadia, and Donna Rawlins. *My Place (The Story of Australia from Now to Then).* Fitzhenry and Whiteside, 1987.

Conflict and Change in Children's Lives
(for Younger Readers)

In this unit students consider the events, both personal and societal, that cause change in children's lives. The books cover a wide range of subjects from moving house to the death of a close friend. Students can begin to see patterns in human experience in different times and places as they consider the causes and effects of change.

Adler, C.S. *Split Sisters*. Aladdin Books, 1990. (Macmillan, 1990.)

Babbitt, Natalie. *The Something*. Sunburst, 1987. (Farrar, Straus, & Giroux, 1987.)
———. *Tuck Everlasting*. Farrar, Straus, & Giroux, 1975.

Bilson, Geoffrey. *Goodbye Sarah*. Kids Can Press, 1984.

Burnett, Frances Hodgson. *The Secret Garden*. Bantam, 1987.

Byars, Betsy. *The Midnight Fox*. Puffin, 1981.

Cameron, Ann. *The Most Beautiful Place in the World*. Knopf, 1988.

Carlsson, Janne. *Camel Bells*. Groundwood, 1989.

Carrick, Carol and Donald. *Stay away from Simon*. Clarion, 1989.

Christopher, Matt. *Catcher with a Glass Arm*. Little, Brown, 1985.
———. *Johnny Long Legs*. Little, Brown, 1988.
———. *Look Who's Playing First Base*. Little, Brown, 1987.

Cleary, Beverly. *Ramona the Brave*. Dell, 1984.

Clifton, Lucille. *Everett Anderson's Goodbye*. Henry Holt, 1988.

Coerr, Eleanor. *Sadako and the Thousand Paper Cranes*. Dell, 1987.
———. *The Josefina Story Quilt*. Harper Trophy, 1986. (HarperCollins, 1989.)

Dalgleish, Alice. *The Courage of Sarah Noble*. Charles Scribner, 1974.

DeJong, Meindert. *The House of Sixty Fathers*. HarperCollins, 1987.

Doyle, Brian. *Angel Square*. Groundwood, 1984.
———. *Easy Avenue*. Groundwood, 1988.
———. *Hey Dad*. Groundwood, 1978.
———. *Up to Low*. Groundwood, 1982.
———. *You Can Pick Me Up at Peggy's Cove*. Groundwood, 1979.

Ellis, Sarah. *The Baby Project*. Groundwood, 1986.
_____. *Next-Door Neighbours*. Groundwood, 1988. (Macmillan, 1990.)

Gardiner, John Reynolds. *Stone Fox*. HarperCollins, 1983.

George, Jean Craighead. *My Side of the Mountain*. Viking, 1988. (Dutton, 1988.)

Kerr, Judith. *When Hitler Stole Pink Rabbit*. Lions, 1974. (Dell, 1987.)

Konigsburg, E. *Journey to an 800 Number*. Dell, 1985.

Lewis, Thomas P. *Hill of Fire*. Harper & Row, 1971. (Harper-Collins, 1987.)

Little, Jean. *Different Dragons*. Puffin, 1989.
_____. *Mama's Going to Buy You a Mockingbird*. Puffin, 1986.

MacLachlan, Patricia. *Sarah, Plain and Tall*. Harper & Row, 1985. (HarperCollins, 1987.)
_____. *Seven Kisses in a Row*. Harper & Row, 1983. (Harper-Collins, 1988.)
_____. *Unclaimed Treasures*. Harper & Row, 1984. (Harper-Collins, 1987.)

Mathis, Sharon Bell. *Sidewalk Story*. Puffin, 1986.

Mattingley, Christobel. *Brave with Ben*. Puffin, 1982.

Naidoo, Beverly. *Journey to Jo'Burg. A South African Story*. Harper & Row, 1986. (HarperCollins, 1988.)

Paperny, Myra. *The Wooden People*. Overlea House, 1987.

Park, Barbara. *The Kid in the Red Jacket*. Knopf, 1988.

Paterson, Katherine. *Bridge to Terabithia*. Harper & Row, 1977. (HarperCollins, 1987.)
_____. *The Great Gilly Hopkins*. Harper & Row, 1987. (Harper-Collins, 1987.)

Porte, Barbara Ann. *Harry in Trouble*. Dell, 1990.
_____. *Harry's Mom*. Dell, 1990.

Sharmat, Marjorie Weinman. *I Don't Care*. Dell, 1979.

Smith, Doris B. *A Taste of Blackberries.* Crowell, 1973. (Harper-Collins, 1988.)

Surat, Michele Maria. *Angel Child, Dragon Child.* Scholastic, 1989.

Varley, Susan. *Badger's Parting Gifts.* Picture Lions, 1985. (Lothrop, 1984.)

Wallace, Ian, and Angela Woods. *The Sandwich.* Kids Can Press, 1975.

Conflict and Change in Children's Lives (for Older Readers)

This bibliography contains titles suitable for use with more experienced readers and students at the older end of our age range. The subject matter is sometimes very mature, though treatment and literary style take into account the age of the readers. In these books students will encounter the traumas of war and conflict through the experiences of the children in the stories. The emphasis is always on hope and the triumph of the human spirit over adversity.

Many of these books contribute to peace studies and the curriculum goals of social awareness and responsibility through their consideration of the futility of trying to settle conflict through violence. Some of the issues raised in the books will need to be treated with great sensitivity, and teachers will find that the Reading Circle becomes a forum for powerful and sometimes emotional discussion.

Not all the books are about war. Some deal with the emotional conflict experienced by children when they are abandoned, treated as outsiders, suffer loss, or face great challenges. Issues of courage, loyalty, and the choices we make in adversity are raised.

Some of the titles are set in nineteenth-century Canada and can be read in conjunction with history or social studies programs that focus on Canadian history in the last century. These books are marked with an asterisk.

Anderson, Rachel. *The War Orphan*. Oxford University Press, 1984. (Richard Drew Publishing, 1987.)

Bell, William. *Forbidden City*. Doubleday, 1990. (Bantam, 1990.)

*Bilson, Geoffrey. *Death over Montreal*. Kids Can Press, 1982.
*_____. *Goodbye Sarah*. Kids Can Press, 1981.
_____. *Hockeybat Harris*. Kids Can Press, 1984.

*Brandis, Marianne. *The Quarter-Pie Window*. The Porcupine's Quill, 1985.
*_____. *The Tinderbox*. The Porcupine's Quill, 1982.

Bunting, Eve. *The Wall*. Clarion Books, 1990. (Houghton Mifflin, 1990.)

Carlsson, Janne. *Camel Bells*. Groundwood, 1989.

Coerr, Eleanor. *Sadako and the Thousand Paper Cranes.* Dell, 1977.

Cooper, Susan. *Dawn of Fear.* Aladdin Books, 1970. (Macmillan, 1989.)

Forbes, Esther. *Johnny Tremain.* Dell, 1987.

Fox, Paula. *One Eyed Cat.* Dell, 1985.
_____. *The Village by the Sea.* Dell, 1990.

Frank, Rudolf. *No Hero for the Kaiser.* J.M. Dent, 1986. (Richard Drew Publishing, 1987.) (Lothrop, 1987.)

*Greenwood, Barbara. *A Question of Loyalty.* Scholastic, 1984.

Harris, Rosemary. *Zed.* Faber & Faber, 1990.

Hautzig, Esther. *The Endless Steppe.* Harper & Row, 1968. (Harper-Collins, 1987.)

Heneghan, Jim. *Promises to Come.* Overlea House, 1988.

Heuck, Sigrid. *The Hideout.* Translated by Rika Lesser. Western Producer Prairie Books, 1986. (Dutton, 1988.)

Hewitt, Marsha, and Claire Mackay. *One Proud Summer.* Puffin, 1989.

Holman, Felice. *Slake's Limbo.* Scribner, 1984. (Macmillan, 1986.)

Hughes, Monica. *Log Jam.* HarperCollins, 1989.

Kasper, Vancy. *Always Ask for a Transfer.* Nelson, 1984.

Kaye, Geraldine. *A Breath of Fresh Air.* Mandarin Teens, 1990. (Trafalgar Square, 1989.)
_____. *Comfort Herself.* Magnet, 1986. (Andre Deutsch, 1985.)

Kerr, Judith. *When Hitler Stole Pink Rabbit.* Lions, 1989. (Dell, 1987.)

Lowry, Lois. *Number the Stars.* Dell, 1990.

*Lunn, Janet. *The Root Cellar.* Puffin, 1985.
*_____. *Shadow in Hawthorn Bay.* Puffin, 1988.

Matas, Carol. *Jesper.* Lester & Orpen Dennys, 1987.
_____. *Lisa.* Lester & Orpen Dennys, 1989.

Moskin, Marietta D. *I Am Rosemarie.* Dell, 1987.

Paterson, Katherine. *Park's Quest.* Puffin, 1989.

Paulsen, Gary. *The Crossing.* Dell, 1990.
_____. *Dogsong.* Puffin, 1987.
_____. *Hatchet.* Puffin, 1988.

Pomerantz, Charlotte. *The Chalk Doll.* J.B. Lippincott, 1989. (HarperCollins, 1989.)

Posell, Elsa. *Homecoming.* William Heinemann Ltd., 1984. (Mammoth, 1989.) (Harcourt Brace Jovanovich, 1987.)

*Reaney, James. *The Boy with an R in His Hand.* The Porcupine's Quill, 1965, 1980, 1984.

*Truss, Jan, and Jack Chambers. *A Very Small Rebellion.* General, 1990.

*Turner, Harold D. *Rebel Gun.* Gage Jean Pac, 1989 (first published as *To Hang a Rebel,* 1977).

Wiseman, David. *Jeremy Visick.* Houghton Mifflin, 1990.

Poetry

COLLECTIONS BY INDIVIDUAL POETS

Ahlberg, Allan. *I Heard It on the Playground.* Illustrated by F. Wegner. Viking, 1989.

Causley, Charles. *Early in the Morning.* Illustrated by Michael Foreman. Viking, 1987.

_____. *Figgie Hobbin.* Illustrated by Jill Bennett. Macmillan, 1979.

_____. *Jack the Treacle Eater.* Illustrated by Charles Keeping. Macmillan, 1987.

Dahl, Roald. *Revolting Rhymes.* Illustrated by Quentin Blake. Puffin, 1984. (Bantam, 1986.)

Dunn, Sonja. *Butterscotch Dreams.* Pembroke, 1987. (Heinemann, 1987.)

_____. *Crackers and Crumbs.* Pembroke, 1990.

Fleischman, Paul. *Joyful Noise: Poems For Two Voices.* Illustrated by Eric Bedows. Harper and Row, 1988. (HarperCollins, 1988.)

Graham, Carolyn. *Fairy Tales.* Oxford University Press, 1988.

_____. *Jazz Chants.* Oxford University Press, 1978.

_____. *Jazz Chants for Children.* Oxford University Press, 1979.

_____. *Small Talk.* Oxford University Press, 1986.

Greenfield, Eloise. *Honey I Love and Other Love Poems.* Harper & Row, 1978. (HarperCollins, 1986.)

Hughes, Ted. *Meet My Folks!* Illustrated by George Adamson. Faber, 1987.

_____. *Moon-Bells and Other Poems.* Illustrated by Felicity Roma Bowers. Bodley Head, 1986.

_____. *Moon-Whales.* Illustrated by Chris Riddell. Faber, 1988.

_____. *Season Songs.* Faber, 1985. (Ultramarine, 1975.)

Lee, Dennis. *Alligator Pie.* Illustrated by Frank Newfeld. Macmillan, 1974.

_____. *Jelly Belly.* Illustrated by Jan Wijngaard. Macmillan, 1983.

_____. *Lizzie's Lion.* Illustrated by Marie-Louise Gay. Stoddart, 1984.

Little, Jean. *Hey World, Here I Am.* Kids Can Press, 1986. (Harper-Collins, 1990.)

McNaughton, Colin. *There's an Awful Lot of Weirdos in Our Neighbourhood.* Walker, 1987.

Nicholls, Judith. *Magic Mirror.* Faber, 1985.
_____. *Midnight Forest.* Faber, 1987.

o'huigan, sean. *The Ghost Horse of the Mounties.* Black Moss Press, 1983. (Godine, 1981.)
_____. *Monsters He Mumbled.* Black Moss Press, 1989.
_____. *Scary Poems for Rotten Kids.* Black Moss Press, 1982.

Owen, Gareth. *Song of the City.* Illustrated by Jonathan Hills. Fontana, 1987.

Prelutsky, Jack. *The New Kid on the Block.* Greenwillow, 1986.
_____. *Ride a Purple Pelican.* Greenwillow, 1987.
_____. *Something Big Has Been Here.* Greenwillow, 1990.
_____. *Under the Blue Umbrella.* Greenwillow, 1990.

Rosen, Michael. *Don't Put the Mustard in the Custard.* Illustrated by Quentin Blake. Andre Deutsch, 1986.
_____. *Quick Let's Get Out of Here.* Andre Deutsch, 1984.
_____. *You Can't Catch Me!* Andre Deutsch, 1981.

ANTHOLOGIES

Booth, David, ed. *Til All The Stars Have Fallen.* Illustrated by K.M. Denton. Kids Can Press, 1989.
_____. *Voices in the Wind: Poems for all Seasons.* Illustrated by Michelle Lemieux. Kids Can Press, 1990. (Morrow, 1990.)

de Paola Tomie, ed. *Book of Poems.* G.P. Putnam, 1980.

Downie, Mary Alice, ed. *The New Wind Has Wings: Poems From Canada.* Illustrated by Barbara Robertson and Elizabeth Cleaver. Oxford University Press, 1984.

Heidebreder, Robert, ed. *Don't Eat Spiders.* Illustrated by Karen Patkau. Oxford University Press, 1985.

Koch, Kenneth, and Kate Farrell, eds. *Talking to the Sun: An Illustrated Anthology of Poems for Young People.* Metropolitan Museum of Art, 1985. (Henry Holt, 1985.)

Lobel, Arnold, ed. *The Random House Book of Mother Goose.* Random House, 1986.

Manguel, Alberto, ed. *Seasons.* Illustrated by Warabe Aska. Doubleday, 1990.

Prelutsky, Jack, ed. *The Walker Book of Poetry for Children.* Illustrated by Arnold Lobel. Walker, 1983.

More Themes

The following short booklists are to help you get started to develop themes around other topics. As always, begin in your own school library and move out from there, visiting the public library and the bookstore. In the first three lists, which are concerned with children from different cultural backgrounds, and with humor, there are books at a range of reading levels, to provide something for everyone in your classroom. The last list suggests novels for more experienced readers on the theme of fantasy and time travel.

WHO ARE WE?
BOOKS ABOUT CHILDREN IN NORTH AMERICA WITH DIFFERENT CULTURAL BACKGROUNDS

Allison, Rosemary. *The Pillow*. Lorimer, 1979.

Canadian Childhoods: Tundra Books Anthology. Tundra, 1989.

Carter, Forrest. *The Education of Little Tree*. University of New Mexico Press, 1986.

Cohen, Barbara. *The Carp in the Bathtub*. Kar-Ben Copies Inc., 1987.

Collins, Judy, and Jane Dyer. *My Father*. Little, Brown, 1989.

Collura, Mary-Ellen Lang. *Winners*. Western Producer Prairie, 1984. (Dial, 1986.)

Doyle, Brian. *Angel Square*. Groundwood, 1984.

Fitzhugh, Louise. *Nobody's Family Is Going to Change*. Farrar, Straus & Giroux, 1986.

Friedman, Ina R. *How My Parents Learned to Eat*. Houghton Mifflin, 1987.

Kasper, Vancy. *Street of Three Directions*. Overlea House, 1988.

Kogawa, Joy. *Naomi's Road*. Oxford University Press, 1988.

Levinson, Riki, and Dennis Luzak. *Our Home Is the Sea*. E.P. Dutton, 1988.

Lim, John. *At Grandmother's House*. Tundra, 1977.

Lim, Sing. *West Coast Chinese Boy*. Tundra, 1991.

Mendez, Phil, and Carole Byard. *The Black Snowman.* Scholastic, 1991.

Paulsen, Gary. *Dogsong.* Puffin, 1987.

Taylor, Mildred. *The Friendship and the Gold Cadillac.* Bantam, 1989.

————. *Roll Of Thunder, Hear My Cry.* Bantam, 1984.

Wallace, Ian. *Chin Chiang and the Dragon's Dance.* Douglas and McIntyre, 1984. (Macmillan, 1984.)

————, and Angela Woods. *The Sandwich.* Kids Can Press, 1975.

Yee, Paul. *Teach Me to Fly, Skyfighter! and Other Stories.* Lorimer, 1983.

CHILDREN IN OTHER PLACES:
STORIES WITH SETTINGS OTHER THAN NORTH AMERICA

Bartholomew, John. *King Fernando.* Puffin, 1988. (Jamaica.)

Berry, James. *A Thief in the Village and Other Stories.* Puffin, 1989. (Orchard, 1988.) (Jamaica.)

Buck, Pearl. *The Big Wave.* HarperCollins, 1986. (Japan.)

Cameron, Ann. *The Most Beautiful Place in the World.* Knopf, 1988. (Guatemala.)

Carlsson, Janne. *Camel Bells.* Groundwood, 1989. (Afghanistan.)

Doppert, Monica. *The Streets Are Free.* Annick, 1985. (Brazil.)

Gray, Nigel, and Philippe Dupasquier. *A Country Far Away.* Anderson Press, 1988. (Orchard, 1991.) (England and the Sudan.)

Grifalconi, Ann. *Darkness and the Butterfly.* Little, Brown, 1987. (Cameroon.)

Kaye, Geraldine. *Comfort Herself.* Magnet, 1988. (Andre Deutsch, 1985.) (England and Ghana.)

Naidoo, Beverly. *Journey To Jo'Burg: A South African Story.* Harper, 1986. (HarperCollins, 1988.) (South Africa.)

Paterson, Katherine. *The Master Puppeteer.* Avon, 1975. (HarperCollins, 1989.) (Japan.)

Ruben, Hilary. *The Calf of the November Cloud.* Pan/Piccolo Books, 1987. (Kenya.)

Thiele, Colin Milton. *Storm Boy*. Rigby/Seal Books, 1976. (Harper-Collins, 1978.) (Australia.)

Ahlberg, Allan. *Woof!* Puffin, 1988.

Babbitt, Natalie. *The Search for Delicious*. Avon, 1974. (Farrar, Straus, & Giroux, 1969.)

Barret, Judi and Ron. *Cloudy with a Chance of Meatballs*. Atheneum, 1982.

Blume, Judy. *Tales of a Fourth Grade Nothing*. Dell, 1976.

Briggs, Raymond. *Fungus the Bogeyman*. Hamish Hamilton, 1977. (Puffin, 1990.)

Brown, Jeff. *Flat Stanley*. Puffin, 1975. (HarperCollins, 1989.)

Byars, Betsy. *The 18th Emergency*. Puffin, 1981. (GK Hall, 1988.)

Cleary, Beverly. *The Mouse and the Motorcycle*. Dell, 1965. (Avon, 1990.)

Dahl, Roald. *James and the Giant Peach*. Bantam, 1978. (Puffin, 1988.)

Doyle, Brian. *You Can Pick Me Up at Peggy's Cove*. Groundwood, 1979.

Fleischman, Sid. *The Whipping Boy*. Greenwillow, 1986. (Troll, 1987.)

Heide, Florence Parry. *The Shrinking of Treehorn*. Holiday, 1971. (Dell, 1979.)

Hoban, Russell, and James Marshall. *Dinner at Alberta's*. Dell, 1980.

Howe, James. *Nighty Nightmare*. Avon, 1988.

King-Smith, Dick. *Saddlebottom*. Puffin, 1987.

Pinkwater, Manus D. *Lizard Music*. Bantam, 1988.

FANTASY AND TIME TRAVEL FOR MORE EXPERIENCED READERS

Alexander, Lloyd. *The Book of Three*. Dell, 1980. (And sequels.)

Boston, Lucy. *The Children of Green Knowe.* Puffin, 1975. (Harcourt Brace Jovanovich, 1989.) (And sequels.)

Christopher, John. *The White Mountains.* 2nd ed. Macmillan, 1988. (And sequels.)

Cooper, Susan. *Over Sea, Under Stone.* Puffin, 1968. (Macmillan, 1989.) (And sequels.)
Cresswell, Helen. *Moondial.* Puffin, 1988. (Macmillan, 1987.)

Garner, Alan. *The Owl Service.* Collins, 1967.

Hughes, Monica. *Keeper of the Isis Light.* Methuen, 1981. (And sequels.)

Le Guin, Ursula. *A Wizard of Earthsea.* Puffin, 1971. (Macmillan, 1991.) (And sequels.)

Lindgren, Astrid. *The Brothers Lionheart.* Puffin, 1985.

Lunn, Janet. *The Root Cellar.* Lester & Orpen Dennys, 1981. (Puffin, 1985.)
_____. *Shadow in Hawthorn Bay.* Lester & Orpen Dennys, 1986. (Puffin, 1988.)

Melling, O.R. *The Druid's Tune.* Puffin, 1983.

Nimmo, Jenny. *The Snow Spider.* E.P. Dutton, 1986. (Troll, 1990.)

Park, Ruth. *Playing Beatie Bow.* Puffin, 1984.

Pearce, Philippa. *Tom's Midnight Garden.* Lippincott, 1958. (Dell, 1991.)

Pearson, Kit. *A Handful of Time.* Puffin, 1991.

Tolkien, J.R.R. *The Hobbit.* Allen & Unwin, 1937. (Houghton Mifflin, 1989.)

Uttley, Alison. *A Traveller in Time.* Faber, 1939.

Recommended Professional Reading for Teachers

Atwell, Nancie. *In the Middle: Reading and Learning with Adolescents*. Heinemann, 1987.

Barton, Bob, and David Booth. *Stories in the Classroom*. Pembroke, 1990. (Heinemann, 1990.)

Benton, Michael, and Geoff Fox. *Teaching Literature Nine to Fourteen*. Oxford University Press, 1985.

Booth, David, Larry Swartz, and Meguido Zola. *Choosing Children's Books*. Pembroke, 1987.

Chambers, Aidan. *Booktalk: Occasional Writing on Literature and Children*. Bodley Head, 1985. (HarperCollins, 1986.)
_____. *Introducing Books to Children*. 2nd ed. Horn Book, 1983.

Cullinan, Bernice, E., ed. *Children's Literature in the Reading Program*. International Reading Association, 1987.

Egoff, Sheila, and Judith Saltman. *The New Republic of Childhood: A Critical Guide to Canadian Children's Literature in English*. Oxford University Press, 1990.

Harste, Jerome C., Kathy G. Short, with Carolyn Burke. *Creating Classrooms for Authors: The Reading Writing Connection*. Heinemann, 1988.

Hazard, Paul. *Books, Children and Men*. Horn Book, 1944. 5th ed., 1983.

Jobe, Ron, and Paula Hart. *Canadian Connections: Experiencing Literature with Children*. Pembroke, 1991.

Johnson, Terry D., and Daphne R. Louis. *Literacy through Literature*. Scholastic, 1987. (Heinemann, 1987.)

Landsberg, Michele. *Michele Landsberg's Guide to Children's Books*. Penguin, 1986.

Meek, Margaret. *How Texts Teach What Readers Learn*. The Thimble Press, 1988.
_____, ed. *The Cool Web: The Pattern of Children's Reading*. Bodley Head, 1977.

Moss, Joy F. *Focus Units in Literature: A Handbook for Elementary School Teachers*. National Council of Teachers of English, 1984.

Paterson, Katherine. *The Gates of Excellence: On Reading and Writing Books for Children.* E.P. Dutton, 1981. (Dutton, 1988.)

Peterson, Ralph, and Maryann Eeds. *Grand Conversations: Literature Groups in Action.* Scholastic, 1990.

Rosenblatt, Louise. *The Reader, the Text, the Poem: The Transactional Theory of the Literary Work.* Southern Illinois Press, 1978.

Short, Kathy Gnagey, and Kathryn Mitchell Pierce. *Talking about Books: Creating Literate Communities.* Heinemann, 1990.

Stott, John C., and Raymond E. Jones. *Canadian Books for Children: A Guide to Authors and Illustrators.* Harcourt Brace Jovanovich, 1988.

Trelease, Jim. *The New Read Aloud Handbook.* Penguin, 1990. (Viking Penguin, 1989.)